PSYCHOTHERAPY
EAST & WEST

PSYCHOTHERAPY
EAST & WEST

ALAN WATTS

New World Library
Novato, California

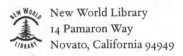

New World Library
14 Pamaron Way
Novato, California 94949

Text design by Tona Pearce Myers

Library of Congress Cataloging-in-Publication Data
Names: Watts, Alan, 1915-1973, author.
Title: Psychotherapy, East and West / Alan Watts.
Description: Novato, CA : New World Library, 2017. |
 Previously published: New York : Vintage Books, 1975. | Includes
 bibliographical references.
Identifiers: LCCN 2016048194 | ISBN 9781608684564 (alk. paper) | ISBN
 9781608684571 (e-book : alk. paper)
Subjects: LCSH: Psychotherapy. | East and West. | Large type books.
Classification: LCC RC480.5 .W33 2017 | DDC 616.89/14--dc23
LC record available at https://lccn.loc.gov/2016048194

First New World Library printing, February 2017
ISBN 978-1-60868-456-4
Ebook ISBN 978-1-60868-457-1
Printed in Canada on 100% postconsumer-waste recycled paper

New World Library is proud to be a Gold Certified Environmentally Responsible Publisher. Publisher certification awarded by Green Press Initiative. www.greenpressinitiative.org

10   9   8   7 6

For Jano

CONTENTS

PREFACE

The subject of this book has been "in the air" for at least thirty years, and during this time there has been an ever-growing discussion of this or that parallel between Western psychotherapy and Eastern philosophy. But thus far no one has attempted, comprehensively, to find some basic design common to the methods and objectives of psychotherapy, on the one hand, and the disciplines of Buddhism, Vedanta, Yoga, and Taoism, on the other. The latter are not, perhaps, psychotherapies in the strict sense, but there is enough resemblance to make the comparison important.

The discussion seems to have begun in the early 1930s, following such works as Richard Wilhelm's translation of a Chinese text, *The Secret of the Golden Flower*, with a long psychological commentary by C. G. Jung (1929), G. R. Heyer's *Der Organismus der Seele* (1932), and Geraldine Coster's *Yoga and Western Psychology* (1934). I have been deeply interested in this fruitful interchange between East and West almost from its beginnings. I also made some contribution to it in a rather immature book called *The Legacy of Asia and Western Man* (1937), and a little later in *The Meaning of Happiness* (1940), which bore the subtitle "The Quest for Freedom of the Spirit in Modern Psychology and in the Wisdom of the East." At that time, almost the only form of psychotherapy which was thus "oriented" was the Jungian. But subsequent developments both in psychotherapy and in our knowledge of Eastern thought have made it possible for us to make much wider and more suggestive comparisons. The same period has also seen an astonishing growth of Western interest in Eastern ways of life, particularly in Zen Buddhism, and the latest contribution to this interchange is the collaboration of Erich Fromm and D. T. Suzuki in *Zen Buddhism and Psychoanalysis* (1960).

My purpose in writing this book is not, however, to sum up or review the development of this discussion. It is rather to give it a new turn. Before the writing began, I saw that there were two main ways of handling the subject. Since I have read almost everything that has been written about it, I saw that I could weave all this material into a kind of critical history of psychiatric interest in Eastern thought, combined with a point-by-point comparison of all the major forms of psychotherapy and all the principal techniques of the Eastern disciplines. But this would have produced an unwieldy volume of rather academic interest; furthermore, such formal studies are not my forte, and I leave them very gladly to those who have the necessary patience and industry. The other way was to describe what I feel to be the most fruitful way in which Eastern and Western psychotherapies can fertilize one another. For not only have they much to learn from each other, but also it seems to me that the comparison brings out hidden and highly important aspects of both. I decided, therefore, to write not a compendium of sober conclusions, but a provocative essay which may jolt both parties to the discussion. For I feel that both are fumbling in the dark, though not without some light. Wonderful as I have found them, I do not believe that the Eastern disciplines are the last word in sacrosanct and immemorial wisdom such that the world must come and sit humbly at the feet of their masters. Nor do I feel that there is a gospel according to Freud, or to Jung, in which the great psychological truths are forever fixed. The aim of this book is not to say the last word on the subject, but to provoke thought and experiment.

My chosen approach to the subject does, however, have the disadvantage of not being able to give adequate mention to all the people who have influenced my thinking, or sufficient recognition to all who have contributed to the discussion. Conversations that were held and books that were read long ago become so much a part of the stream of one's own thinking that it is impossible, sometimes, to say which ideas are one's own and which are borrowed. This book does not therefore make explicit what may have come from my early reading of such speculative and adventurous therapists as Trigant Burrow, Georg Groddeck, and my friend Eric Graham Howe. It does not specify what I have gained over the years from discussion of its main theme with Professor Frederic Spiegelberg, of Stanford University, or with Dr. Lillian Baker and the late Dr. Charles G. Taylor, both Jungian analysts. Nor does it acknowledge the contributions which have been made to the subject by Medard Boss, Hubert Benoit, Henry Dicks, and Lili Abegg, in Europe; by Shoma Morita, Takehisa Kora, and Akihisa Kondo, in Japan; or by Karen Horney, Harold Kellman, Joseph Campbell, Margaret Rioch, and many others, in the United States.

But the reader will quickly recognize, in the book's underlying philosophy of the universe as organic and transactional, my debt to A. N. Whitehead, Joseph Needham, L. L. Whyte, A. F. Bentley, and the Gestalt psychologists. If he has read my other books, he will also see the more recent influence of what I must call, to distinguish them from the neo-Freudians like Horney and Fromm, the "meta-Freudians" Norman O. Brown and Herbert Marcuse. He will also note my increasing respect for the "communication psychology" of Gregory Bateson and his associates, particularly Jay Haley, which goes hand in hand with my growing preference for discussing these matters in a language that is more scientific and less metaphysical.

He will find, therefore, that I place more weight upon the connection of the Eastern disciplines with forms of psychotherapy whose philosophy is social, interpersonal, and communicational than with those which stress "the unconscious" and its archetypal images. Even though the discussion of this interchange between East and West has so largely been carried on by those who follow the latter trend, I cannot help feeling that it is becoming more and more of a backwater in the development of Western psychiatry, despite the debt which we shall always owe to Freud. Psychoanalysis in particular and "depth psychology" in general seem to me to be increasingly out of touch with all that has been going on in the sciences of human behavior during the last thirty years, and many of us are wondering seriously how long it will be possible for psychology, the study of an alleged psyche, to remain a department of science.

In addition to the influences mentioned above, this book has not been prepared without a great deal of discussion with persons actively engaged in psychotherapy. During the past few years I have had the privilege of conducting seminars upon its subject and of being a guest lecturer at many medical schools, hospitals, and psychiatric institutes — including the Yale Medical School, the Langley-Porter Clinic of the University of California, the C. G. Jung Institute in Zürich, the Washington School of Psychiatry, the Palo Alto Veterans' Hospital, the Stanford Medical School, and many state psychiatric hospitals. My thanks are due to all those responsible for these opportunities.

Alan W. Watts
San Francisco, 1960

I. Psychotherapy
and Liberation

If we look deeply into such ways of life as Buddhism and Taoism, Vedanta and Yoga, we do not find either philosophy or religion as these are understood in the West. We find something more nearly resembling psychotherapy. This may seem surprising, for we think of the latter as a form of science, somewhat practical and materialistic in attitude, and of the former as extremely esoteric religions concerned with regions of the spirit almost entirely out of this world. This is because the combination of our unfamiliarity with Eastern cultures and their sophistication gives them an aura of mystery into which we project fantasies of our own making. Yet the basic aim of these ways of life is something of quite astonishing simplicity, besides which all the complications of reincarnation and psychic powers, of superhuman mahatmas, and of schools for occult technology are a smoke screen in which the credulous inquirer can lose himself indefinitely. In fairness it should be added that the credulous inquirer may be Asian as well as Western, though the former has seldom the peculiarly highbrow credulity of the Western fancier of esotericism. The smoke is beginning to clear, but for a long time its density has hidden the really important contributions of the Eastern mind to psychological knowledge.

The main resemblance between these Eastern ways of life and Western psychotherapy is in the concern of both with bringing about changes of consciousness, changes in our ways of feeling our own existence and our relation to human society and the natural world. The psychotherapist has, for the most part, been interested in changing the consciousness of peculiarly disturbed individuals. The disciplines of Buddhism and Taoism are, however, concerned with changing the consciousness of normal, socially adjusted people. But it is increasingly apparent to psychotherapists that the normal state of consciousness in our culture is both the context and the breeding ground of mental disease. A complex of societies of vast material wealth bent on mutual destruction is anything but a condition of social health.

Nevertheless, the parallel between psychotherapy and, as I have called them,[1] the Eastern "ways of liberation" is not exact, and one of the most important differences is suggested by the prefix *psycho-*. Historically, Western psychology has directed itself to the study of the psyche, or mind, as a clinical entity, whereas Eastern cultures have not categorized mind and matter, soul and body, in the same way as the Western. But Western psychology has to some extent so outgrown its historical origins as to become dissatisfied with the very term "psychological" as describing a major field of human behavior. It is not that it has become possible, as Freud himself once hoped, to reduce psychology to neurology and mind to body. It is not that for the entity "mind" we can substitute the entity "nervous system." It is rather that psychology cannot stand aloof from the whole revolution in scientific description which has been going on in the twentieth century, a revolution in which conceptions of entities and "stuffs," whether mental or material, have become obsolete. Whether it is describing chemical changes or biological forms, nuclear structures or human behavior, the language of modern science is simply concerned with changing patterns of relationship.

Perhaps this revolution has affected physics and biology far more deeply than psychology and as yet the theoretical ideas of psychoanalysis remain untouched. The common speech and the common sense of even educated society has been so little affected that it is still hard to convey in some nonmathematical language what has happened. It seems an affront to common sense that we can describe the world as patterns of relationship without needing to ask what "stuff" these patterns are "made of." For when the scientist investigates matter or stuff, he describes what he finds in terms of structured pattern. When one comes to think of it, what other terms could he use? The sensation of stuff arises only when we are confronted with patterns so confused or so closely knit that we cannot make them out. To the naked eye a distant galaxy looks like a solid star and a piece of steel like a continuous and impenetrable mass of matter. But when we change the level of magnification, the galaxy assumes the clear structure of a spiral nebula and the piece of steel turns out to be a system of electrical impulses whirling in relatively vast spaces. The idea of stuff expresses no more than the experience of coming to a limit at which our senses or our instruments are not fine enough to make out the pattern.

Something of the same kind happens when the scientist investigates any unit of pattern so distinct to the naked eye that it has been considered a separate entity. He finds that the more carefully he observes and describes it, the more he is *also* describing the environment in which it moves and other patterns to which it seems inseparably related. As Teilhard de Chardin has so well expressed it,[2] the isolation of individual, atomic patterns "is merely an intellectual dodge."

> Considered in its physical, concrete reality, the stuff [sic] of the universe cannot divide itself but, as a kind of gigantic "atom," it forms in its totality...the only real indivisible.... The farther and more deeply we penetrate into matter, by means of increasingly powerful methods, the more we are confounded by the interdependence of its parts.... It is impossible to cut into this network, to isolate a portion without it becoming frayed and unravelled at all its edges.

In place of the inarticulate cohesion of mere stuff we find the articulate cohesion of inseparably interconnected patterns.

The effect of this upon the study of human behavior is that it becomes impossible to separate psychological patterns from patterns that are sociological, biological, or ecological. Departments of knowledge based upon what now appear to be crude and primitive divisions of nature begin to coalesce into such awkwardly named hybrids as neuropsychiatry, sociobiology, biophysics, and geopolitics. At a certain depth of specialization the divisions of scientific knowledge begin to run together because they are far enough advanced to see that the world itself runs together, however clear-cut its parts may have seemed to be. Hence the ever-increasing discussion of the need for a "unified science" and for a descriptive language common to all departments of science. Hence, too, the growing importance of the very science of description, of communication, of the patterns of signs and signals, which represents and elucidates the pattern of the world.

Although the ancient cultures of Asia never attained the rigorously exact physical knowledge of the modern West, they grasped in principle many things which are only now occurring to us.[3] Hinduism and Buddhism are impossible to classify as religions, philosophies, sciences, or even mythologies, or again as amalgamations of all four, because departmentalization is foreign to them even in so basic a form as the separation of the spiritual and the material. Hinduism, like Islam and Judaism, is really a whole culture, though the same cannot be said of Buddhism. Buddhism, in common with such aspects of Hinduism as Vedanta and Yoga, and with Taoism in China, is not a culture but a critique of culture, an enduring nonviolent revolution, or "loyal opposition," to the culture with which it is involved. This gives these ways of liberation something in common with psychotherapy beyond the interest in changing states of consciousness. For the task of the psychotherapist is to bring about a reconciliation between individual feeling and social norms without, however, sacrificing the integrity of the individual. He tries to help the individual to be himself and to go it alone without giving unnecessary offense to his community, to be in the world (of social convention) but not of the world. A Chinese Buddhist text describes the sage in words that strongly suggest Riesman's "inner-directed" or Maslow's "self-actualizing" personality:

> *He walks always by himself, goes about always by himself;*
> *Every perfect one saunters along one and the same passage of*
> *Nirvana;*
> *His tone is classical, his spirit is transparent, his airs are*
> *naturally elevated,*

His features are rather gaunt, his bones are firm, he pays no attention to others.[4]

From Freud onward, psychotherapy has been concerned with the violence done to the human organism and its functions by social repression. Whenever the therapist stands with society, he will interpret his work as adjusting the individual and coaxing his "unconscious drives" into social respectability. But such "official psychotherapy" lacks integrity and becomes the obedient tool of armies, bureaucracies, churches, corporations, and all agencies that require individual brainwashing. On the other hand, the therapist who is really interested in helping the individual is forced into social criticism. This does not mean that he has to engage directly in political revolution; it means that he has to help the individual in liberating himself from various forms of social conditioning, which includes liberation from hating this conditioning — hatred being a form of bondage to its object. But from this point of view the troubles and symptoms from which the patient seeks relief, and the unconscious factors behind them, cease to be merely psychological. They lie in the whole pattern of his relationships with other people and, more particularly, in the social institutions by which these relationships are governed: the rules of communication employed by the culture or group. These include the conventions of language and law, of ethics and aesthetics, of status, role, and identity, and of cosmology, philosophy, and religion. For this whole social complex is what provides the individual's conception of himself, his state of consciousness, his very feeling of existence. What is more, it provides the human organism's idea of its individuality, which can take a number of quite different forms.

Seeing this, the psychotherapist must realize that his science, or art, is misnamed, for he is dealing with something far more extensive than a psyche and its private troubles. This is just what so many psychotherapists are recognizing and what, at the same time, makes the Eastern ways of liberation so pertinent to their work. For they are dealing with people whose distress arises from what may be termed *maya*, to use the Hindu-Buddhist word whose exact meaning is not merely "illusion" but the entire world-conception of a culture, considered as illusion in the strict etymological sense of a play (Latin, *ludere*). The aim of a way of liberation is not the destruction of *maya* but seeing it for what it is, or seeing through it. Play is not to be taken seriously, or, in other words, ideas of the world and of oneself which are social conventions and institutions are not to be confused with reality. The rules of communication are not necessarily the rules of the universe, and man is not the role or identity which society thrusts upon him. For when a man no longer confuses himself with the definition of himself that others have given him, he is at once universal and unique. He is universal by virtue of the inseparability of his organism from the cosmos. He is unique in that he is just *this* organism and not any stereotype of role, class, or identity assumed for the convenience of social communication.

There are many reasons why distress comes from confusing this social *maya* with reality. There is direct conflict between what the individual organism is and what others say it is and expect it to be. The rules of social communication often contain contradictions which lead to impossible dilemmas in thought, feeling, and action. Or it may be that confusion of oneself with a limiting and impoverished view of one's role or identity creates feelings of isolation, loneliness, and alienation. The multitudinous differences between individuals and their social contexts lead to as many ways of seeking relief from these conflicts. Some seek it in the psychoses and neuroses which lead to psychiatric treatment, but for the most part release is sought in the socially permissible orgies of mass entertainment, religious fanaticism, chronic sexual titillation, alcoholism, war — the whole sad list of tedious and barbarous escapes.

Naturally, then, it is being said that the need for psychotherapy goes far beyond that of those who are clinically psychotic or neurotic, and for many years now increasing numbers of people have been receiving psychotherapy who would formerly have sought counsel from a minister of religion or a sympathetic friend. But no one has yet discovered how to apply psychotherapy on a mass basis. Trained therapists exist in a ratio of about one to eight thousand of the population, and the techniques of psychotherapy are lengthy and expensive. Its growing popularity is due in large measure to the prestige of science and thus of the therapist as a scientific rather than religious soul doctor. Yet I know of a few reputable psychiatrists who will not admit, at least in private, that their profession is still far from being a science. To begin with, there is no generally accepted theory or even terminology of the science, but rather a multiplicity of conflicting theories and divergent techniques. Our knowledge of neurology, if this should prove to be the basis of psychiatry, is as yet extremely limited. To make things worse, there is still no clear evidence that psychotherapy is anything more than a hit-or-miss placebo, and, save in the case of psychotic symptoms that can be controlled by certain drugs, there is no sure way of distinguishing its "cures" from spontaneous remission. And some of its techniques, including lobotomy and shock treatment, are nothing but measures of sheer desperation.

Nevertheless, the profession is on the whole a patient and devoted fraternity, receptive to all manner of new ideas and experiments. Even if it does not know what sense to make of it, an enormous amount of detailed information has been collected, and there is a growing realization that, to make any progress, psychiatry must ally itself more closely with neurology and biology on one side and with sociology and anthropology on the other. We must ask, then, to what other milieu in our society we can look for anything to be done about the distress of the individual in his conflict with social institutions which are self-contradictory, obsolete, or needlessly restricting — including, it must be repeated, the current notion of the individual himself, of the skin-encapsulated ego.

That many people now consult the psychotherapist rather than the minister is not due simply to the fact that science has greater prestige than religion. Many Protestant and Jewish theological seminaries include courses of instruction in "pastoral psychiatry," comprising periods of internship in mental hospitals. Furthermore, religion has been so liberalized that in all metropolitan and in many rural areas one has not far to go to find a minister who will listen to no matter what individual difficulty with the greatest sympathy and generosity, and often with considerable intelligence. But what hinders the minister in resolving conflicts between the individual and social institutions is precisely his own role. He represents a church, a community, and almost without exception religious communities work to establish social institutions and not to see through them. This is not to say that most religious groups abstain from social criticism, since this would be very far from true. Most religious groups oppose *some* social institutions quite vigorously, but at the same time they inculcate others without understanding their conventional nature. For those which they inculcate they claim the authority of the will of God or the laws of nature, thus making

it extremely difficult for their members to see that social institutions are simply rules of communication which have no more
universal validity than, say, the rules of a particular grammar.
Furthermore, however sympathetic the minister of religion may
be, in the back of his mind there is almost always the desire to
bring the individual back into the fold of his church.

The Jewish-Christian idea of salvation means precisely
membership in a community, the Communion of Saints. Ide-
ally and theoretically the Church as the Body of Christ is the
entire universe, and because in Christ "there is neither Greek
nor Jew, bond nor free," membership in Christ *could* mean liberation from *maya* and its categories. It could mean that one's
conventional definition and classification is not one's real self,
that "I live, yet no longer I; but Christ lives in me." But in
practice it means nothing of the kind, and, for that matter, one
hears little even of the theory. In practice it means accepting the
religion or bondage of the Christian subgroup, taking its particular system of conventions and definitions to be the most serious
realities. Now one of the most important Christian conventions
is the view of man as what I have called the "skin-encapsulated
ego," the separate soul and its fleshy vehicle together consti-
tuting a personality which is unique and ultimately valuable in
the sight of God. This view is undoubtedly the historical basis
of the Western style of individuality, giving us the sensation of
ourselves as isolated islands of consciousness confronted with
objective experiences which are quite "other." We have developed this sensation to a particularly acute degree. But the system
of conventions which inculcates this sensation *also* requires this
definitively isolated ego to act as the member of a body and to
submit without reserve to the social pattern of the church. The
tension so generated, however interesting at times, is in the long

run as unworkable as any other flat self-contradiction. It is a perfectly ideal context for breeding psychosis. Yet, as we shall see, it would also be an ideal context for therapy if responsible religious leaders were aware of the contradiction and did not take it seriously. In other words, the minister might become an extraordinarily helpful person if he could see through his own religion. But his training and his economic situation do not encourage him to do so, and therefore the psychotherapist is in a more advantageous position.

Thus far, then, we have seen that psychotherapy and the ways of liberation have two interests in common: first, the transformation of consciousness, of the inner feeling of one's own existence; and second, the release of the individual from forms of conditioning imposed upon him by social institutions. What are the useful means of exploring these resemblances so as to help the therapist in his work? Should he take practical instruction in Yoga, or spend time in a Japanese Zen monastery — adding yet more years of training to medical school, psychiatric residency, or training analysis? I do not feel that this is the point at all. It is rather that even a theoretical knowledge of other cultures helps us to understand our own, because we can attain some clarity and objectivity about our own social institutions by comparing them with others. It helps us to distinguish between social fictions, on the one hand, and natural patterns and relationships, on the other. If, then, there are in other cultures disciplines having something in common with psychotherapy, a theoretical knowledge of their methods, objectives, and principles may enable the psychotherapist to get a better perspective upon what he himself is doing.

This he needs rather urgently. For we have seen that at the present time psychology and psychiatry are in a state of great theoretical confusion. It may sound strange to say that most of this confusion is due to unconscious factors, for is it not the particular business of these sciences to understand "the unconscious"? But the unconscious factors bearing upon psychotherapy go far beyond the traumas of infancy and the repressions of anger and sexuality. For example, the psychotherapist carries on his work with an almost wholly unexamined "philosophical unconscious." He tends to be ignorant, by reason of his highly specialized training, not only of the contemporary philosophy of science but also of the hidden metaphysical premises which underlie all the main forms of psychological theory. Unconscious metaphysics tends to be bad metaphysics. What, then, if the metaphysical presuppositions of psychoanalysis are invalid, or if its theory depends on discredited anthropological ideas of the nineteenth century? Throughout his writings Jung insists again and again that he speaks as a scientist and physician and not as a metaphysician. "Our psychology," he writes, "is...a science of mere phenomena without any metaphysical implications." It "treats all metaphysical claims and assertions as mental phenomena, and regards them as statements about the mind and its structure that derive ultimately from certain unconscious dispositions."[5] But this is a whopping metaphysical assumption in itself. The difficulty is that man can hardly think or act at all without some kind of metaphysical premise, some basic axiom which he can neither verify nor fully define. Such axioms are like the rules of games: some give ground for interesting and fruitful plays and some do not, but it is always important to understand as clearly as possible what the rules are. Thus the rules of tick-tack-toe are not as fruitful as those of chess, and what if the axioms of psychoanalysis resemble the former instead of the latter? Would this not put the science back to the level of mathematics when geometry was only Euclidean?

Unconscious factors in psychotherapy include also the

social and ecological contexts of patient and therapist alike, and these tend to be ignored in a situation where two people are closeted together in private. As Norman O. Brown has put it:

> There is a certain loss of insight in the tendency of psychoanalysis to isolate the individual from culture. Once we recognize the limitations of talk from the couch, or rather, once we recognize that talk from the couch is still an activity in culture, it becomes plain that there is nothing for the psychoanalyst to analyze except these cultural projections — the world of slums and telegrams and newspapers — and thus psychoanalysis fulfills itself only when it becomes historical and cultural analysis.[6]

Is not this a way of saying that what needs to be analyzed or clarified in an individual's behavior is the way in which it reflects the contradictions and confusions of the culture?

Now cultural patterns come to light and hidden metaphysical assumptions become clear only to the degree that we can step outside the cultural or metaphysical systems in which we are involved by comparing them with others. There are those who argue that this is simply impossible, that our impressions of other cultures are always hopelessly distorted by our own conditioning. But this is almost a cultural solipsism, and it is equivalent to saying that we can never really be in communication with another person. If this be true, all study of foreign languages and institutions, and even all discourse with other individuals, is nothing but extending the pattern of one's own ignorance. As a metaphysical assumption there is no way of disproving it, but it offers nothing in the way of a fruitful development.

The positive aspect of liberation as it is understood in the Eastern ways is precisely freedom of play. Its negative aspect is criticism of premises and rules of the "social game" which restrict this freedom and do not allow what we have called fruitful development. The Buddhist *Nirvana* is defined as release from *samsara*, literally the Round of Birth and Death, that is, from life lived in a vicious circle, as an endlessly repetitious attempt to solve a false problem. *Samsara* is therefore comparable to attempts to square the circle, trisect the angle, or construct a mechanism of perpetual motion. A puzzle which has no solution forces one to go over the same ground again and again until it appears that the question which it poses is nonsense. This is why the neurotic person keeps repeating his behavior patterns — always unsuccessful because he is trying to solve a false problem, to make sense of a self-contradiction. If he cannot see that the problem itself is nonsense, he may simply retreat into psychosis, into the paralysis of being unable to act at all. Alternatively, the "psychotic break" may also be an illegitimate burst into free play out of sheer desperation, not realizing that the problem is impossible not because of overwhelming difficulty, but because it is meaningless.

If, then, there is to be fruitful development in the science of psychotherapy, as well as in the lives of those whom it intends to help, it must be released from the unconscious blocks, unexamined assumptions, and unrealized nonsense problems which lie in its social context. Again, one of the most powerful instruments for this purpose is intercultural comparison, especially with highly complex cultures like the Chinese and Indian, which have grown up in relative isolation from our own, and especially with attempts that have been made within those cultures to find liberation from their own patterns. It is hard to imagine anything more constructive to the psychotherapist than the opportunity which this affords. But to make use of it he must overcome the habitual notion that he has nothing to learn from "prescientific" disciplines, for in the case of psychotherapy this may be a matter of the pot calling the kettle black. In any event, there is no question here of his adopting Buddhist or Taoist practices in the sense of becoming converted to a religion. If the Westerner is to understand and employ the Eastern ways of liberation at all, it is of the utmost importance that he keep his scientific wits about him; otherwise there is the morass of esoteric romanticism which awaits the unwary.

But today, past the middle of the twentieth century, there is no longer much of a problem in advocating a hearing for Eastern ideas. The existing interest in them is already considerable, and they are rapidly influencing our thinking by their own force, even though there remains a need for much interpretation, clarification, and assimilation. Nor can we commend their study to psychotherapists as if this were something altogether new. It is now thirty years since Jung wrote:

> When I began my life-work in the practice of psychiatry and psychotherapy, I was completely ignorant of Chinese philosophy, and it is only later that my professional experiences have shown me that in my technique I had been unconsciously led along that secret way which for centuries has been the preoccupation of the best minds of the East.[7]

An equivalence between Jung's analytical psychology and the ways of liberation must be accepted with some reservations, but it is important that he felt it to exist. Though the interest began with Jung and his school, suspect among other schools for its alleged "mysticism," it has gone far beyond, so much so that it would be a fair undertaking to document the discussions of Eastern ideas which have appeared in psychological books and journals during the past few years.[*]

---

[*] Under the heading "Contributions from Related Fields," the recent *American Handbook of Psychiatry* (New York: Basic Books, 1959) contains full articles by Eilhard von Domarus on Oriental "religions" and by Avrum Ben-Avi on Zen Buddhism.

The level at which Eastern thought and its insights may be of value to Western psychology has been admirably stated by Gardner Murphy, a psychologist who, incidentally, can hardly be suspected of the taint of Jung's "mysticism." He writes:

> If, moreover, we are serious about understanding all we can of personality, its integration and disintegration, we must understand the meaning of depersonalization, those experiences in which individual self-awareness is abrogated and the individual melts into an awareness which is no longer anchored upon selfhood. Such experiences are described by Hinduism in terms of the ultimate unification of the individual with the atman, the superindividual cosmic entity which transcends both selfhood and materiality....Some men desire such experiences; others dread them. Our problem here is not their desirability, but the light which they throw on the relativity of our present-day psychology of personality....Some other mode of personality configuration, in which self-awareness is less emphasized or even lacking, may prove to be the general (or the fundamental).[8]

It is of course a common misapprehension that the change of personal consciousness effected in the Eastern ways of liberation is "depersonalization" in the sense of regression to a primitive or infantile type of awareness. Indeed, Freud designated the longing for return to the oceanic consciousness of the womb as the *Nirvana*-principle, and his followers have persistently confused all ideas of transcending the ego with mere loss of "ego strength." This attitude flows, perhaps, from the imperialism of Western Europe in the nineteenth century, when it became convenient to regard Indians and Chinese as backward and benighted heathens desperately in need of improvement by colonization.

It cannot be stressed too strongly that liberation does not involve the loss or destruction of such conventional concepts as the ego; it means seeing through them — in the same way that we can use the idea of the equator without confusing it with a physical mark upon the surface of the earth. Instead of falling below the ego, liberation surpasses it. Writing without apparent knowledge of Buddhism or Vedanta, A. F. Bentley put it thus:

> Let no quibble of skepticism be raised over this questioning of the existence of the individual. Should he find reason for holding that he does not exist in the sense indicated, there will in that fact be no derogation from the reality of what does exist. On the contrary, there will be increased recognition of reality. For the individual can be banished only by showing a plus of existence, not by alleging a minus. If the individual falls it will be because the real life of men, when it is widely enough investigated, proves too rich for him, not because it proves too poverty-stricken.[9]

One has only to look at the lively and varied features and the wide-awake eyes of Chinese and Japanese paintings of the Great Zen masters to see that the ideal of personality here shown is anything but the collective nonentity or the weakling ego dissolving back into the womb.

Our mistake has been to suppose that the individual is honored and his uniqueness enhanced by emphasizing his separation from the surrounding world, or his eternal difference in essence from his Creator. As well honor the hand by lopping it from the arm! But when Spinoza said that "The more we know of particular things, the more we know of God," he was anticipating our discovery that the richer and more articulate our picture of man and of the world becomes, the more we are aware of its relativity and of the interconnection of all its patterns in an undivided whole. The psychotherapist is perfectly in accord with the ways of liberation in describing the goal of therapy as individuation (Jung), self-actualization (Maslow), functional autonomy (Allport), or creative selfhood (Adler), but every plant that is to come to its full fruition must be embedded in the soil, so that as its stem ascends the whole earth reaches up to the sun.

II. Society and Sanity

Though it cannot as yet be shown that a society is a body of people in the same way that a man is a body of cells, it is clear that any social group is something more than the sum of its members. People do not live in mere juxtaposition. To sum is to collect things together in a one-to-one correspondence with a series of numbers, and the relationship between 1 and 2 and 3 and 4 is so simple that it does not begin to resemble the relationship of people living together. A society is people living together in a certain pattern of behavior — a pattern which makes such physical traces as roads and the structure of towns, codes of law and language, tools and artifacts, all of which lay down "channels" determining the future behavior of the group. Moreover, a society is not "made up" of people in the same way that a house is composed of bricks, or even in the same way that an army is gathered together by recruitment. Strictly speaking, society is not so much a thing as a process of action which is really indistinguishable from human beings and animals, and from life itself. That no human organism exists without male and female parents is already society.

As a pattern of behavior, society is above all a system of people in communication maintained by *consistent* action. To keep the system going, what is done has to be consistent with what has been done. The pattern is recognizable as a pattern because it goes ahead with reference to its own past; it is just this that establishes what we call order and identity, a situation in which trees do not suddenly turn into rabbits and in which one man does not suddenly behave like another so that we do not know who he is. "Who" is consistent behavior. System, pattern, coherence, order, agreement, identity, and consistency are all in a way synonymous. But in a pattern so mobile and volatile as human society, maintaining consistency of action and communication is not easy. It requires the most elaborate agreements as to what the pattern is, or, to put it in another way, as to what are the rules, the consistencies, of the system. Without agreement as to the rules of playing together there is no game. Without agreement as to the use of words, signs, and gestures there is no communication.

The maintenance of society would be simple enough if human beings were content just to survive. In this case they would be simply animals, and it would be enough to eat, sleep, and reproduce. But if these are their basic needs, human beings go about getting them in the most complicated way imaginable. If what must be done to survive is work, it would seem that the main concern of human beings is to play, yet at the same time pretending that most of such play is work. When one comes to think of it, the boundary between work and play is vague and changeable. Both are work in the sense that they expend energy; but if work is what *must* be done to survive, may we not ask, "But is it really necessary to survive? Is not survival, the continuation of the consistent pattern of the organism, a form of play?" We must be careful of the anthropomorphism which asserts that animals hunt and eat *in order* to survive, or that a sunflower turns *in order* to keep its face to the sun. There is no scientific reason to suppose that there are such things as instincts for survival or for pleasure. When we say that an organism *likes* to go on living, or that it goes on living because it likes it, what evidence is there for this "like" except that it does in fact go on living — until it doesn't? Similarly, to say that we always choose what we prefer says no more than that we always choose what we choose. If there is a basic urge to live, there must also, as Freud thought, be a basic urge to die. But language and thought are cleaner without these ghostly instincts, urges, and necessities. As Wittgenstein says, "A necessity for one thing to happen because another has happened does not exist. There is only *logical* necessity."[10]

An enduring organism is simply one that is consistent with its environment. Its climate and its food agree with it; its pattern assimilates them, eliminating what does not agree, and this consistent motion, this transformation of food and air into the pattern of the organism, is what we call its existence. There is no mysterious necessity for this to continue or discontinue. To say that the organism *needs* food is only to say that it *is* food. To say that it eats *because* it is hungry is only to say that it eats when it is ready to eat. To say that it dies because it cannot find food is only another way of saying that its death is the same thing as its ceasing to be consistent with the environment. The so-called causal explanation of an event is only the description of the same event in other words. To quote Wittgenstein again, "At the basis of the whole modern view of the world lies the illusion that the so-called laws of nature are the explanations of natural phenomena."[11]

More complex organisms, such as human beings, are more complex consistencies, more complex transformations of the environment. Not only are they patterns of transforming food, but their agreement or consistency with the environment changes nuclear vibrations into sound and light, weight and color, taste and smell, temperature and texture, until finally they generate elaborate patterns of signs and symbols of great interior consistency. When these mesh with the environment it becomes possible to describe the world in terms of sign patterns. The world is thus transformed into thought in the same way that food was transformed into body. The agreement or consistency of body pattern or thought pattern with the pattern of the world goes on as long as it goes on. To say *why* it starts or stops is only to describe particular consistencies or inconsistencies.

To say that there is no necessity for things to happen as they do is perhaps another way of saying that the world is play. But this idea is an affront to common sense because the basic rule of human societies is that one *must* be consistent. If you want to belong to our society, you must play our game — or, simply, *if* we are going to be consistent, we *must* be consistent. The conclusion is substituted for the premise. But this is understandable because, as we have seen, human society is so complex and volatile that consistency is difficult to maintain. Children keep slipping out of the patterns of behavior that we try to impose upon them, and for this and similar reasons our social conventions have to be maintained by force. The first rule of the game, put in another way, is that the game must continue, that the survival of the society is necessary. But we must not lose sight of the fact that the consistencies or regularities of nature are patterns that do occur, not patterns that must occur. Natural events do not obey commandments in the same way that human beings obey the law.*

Or put in still other words, the first rule of the game is that this game is *serious*, i.e., is not a game. This might be called the primordial "repression." By this I do not mean that it is an event at the temporal beginnings of human life, but rather that it may be our most deeply ingrained social attitude. But just as soon as we feel that certain things, such as survival, are serious necessities, life becomes problematic in a very special sense quite different from, say, the problems of chess or of science. Life and problem become the same; the human situation becomes a predicament for which there is no solution. Man then behaves as a self-frustrating organism, and this behavior can be seen in many different ways. For example, one of our greatest assets for survival is our sense of time, our marvelously sensitive memory, which enables us to predict the future from the pattern of the past. Yet awareness of time ceases to be an asset when concern for the future makes it almost impossible to live fully in the present, or when increasing knowledge of the future makes it increasingly certain that beyond a brief span we have no future. If, too, man's growing sensitivity requires that he become more and more aware of himself as an individual, if social institutions are designed more and more to foster the unique person, not only are we in great danger of overpopulating but also we are

---

* In his superb essay "Human Law and the Laws of Nature," in Vol. 2 of *Science and Civilization in China*, Joseph Needham has shown that, largely because of Taoist influence, Chinese thought has never confused the order of nature with the order of law. As a way of liberation Taoism, of course, brings to light the manner in which men project their social institutions upon the structure of the universe.

betting and concentrating upon man in his most vulnerable and impermanent form.*

This self-frustrating activity is *samsara*, the vicious circle from which the ways of liberation propose release. Release depends upon becoming aware of that primordial repression which is responsible for the feeling that life is a problem, that it is serious, that it *must* go on. It has to be seen that the problem we are trying to solve is absurd. But this means far more than mere resignation to fate, far more than the stoic despair of recognizing that human life is a losing battle with the chaos of nature. That would amount only to seeing that the problem has no solution. We should then simply withdraw from it and sit aloof in a kind of collective psychosis. The point is not that the problem has no solution, but that it is so meaningless that it need not be felt as a problem. To quote Wittgenstein again:

> For an answer which cannot be expressed the question too cannot be expressed. *The riddle* does not exist. If a question can be put at all, then it *can* also be answered....For doubt can only exist where there is a question; a question only where there is an answer, and this only where something can be *said*. We feel that even if *all possible* scientific questions be answered, the problems of life have still not been touched at all. Of course there is then no question left, and just this is the answer. The solution of the problem of life is seen in the vanishing of this problem. (Is not this the reason why men to whom after long doubting the sense of life became clear, could not then say wherein this sense consisted?)[12]

---

* This is perhaps comparable to a shift in the level of magnification so as to observe the individual members of a colony of microorganisms instead of its overall behavior.

When a psychiatrist asked a Zen master how he dealt with neurotic people he replied, "I trap them!" "And just how do you trap them?" "I get them where they can't ask any more questions!"

But the idea that human life need not be felt as a problem is so unfamiliar and seemingly implausible that we must go more deeply into the social origins of the problematic feeling. In the first place, the opposition of human order to natural chaos is false. To say that there is no natural necessity is *not* to say that there is no natural order, no pattern or consistency, in the physical world. After all, man himself is part of the physical world, and so is his logic. But it should not be hard to see that the kind of order which we call logical or causal necessity is a subtype of order, a kind of order which appears in the world but is not characteristic of it as a whole. Similarly, the order of the rational integers 1, 2, 3, etc., is in the world, but mathematics would be a poor tool for describing the world if it were confined to simple arithmetic. We could say that the order of probability describes the world better than the order of causality. This is the same sort of truth as that a man with a saw can cut wood better than a man with a stone ax. The world is to us as we have means of assimilating it: patterns of thought-language in whose terms we can describe it. Yet these patterns are physical events, just as much as those which they describe. The point is surely that the world has no *fixed* order. We could almost say that the world is ordering itself ever more subtly both by means of and as the behaviors of living organisms.

We saw that primitive organisms consist with their environments by the transformation of food, etc., into the patterns of their bodies. This can be put the other way around by saying that environments consist with organisms by being of such a nature that this is possible. Ecologists speak of the evolution of the environment as well as the evolution of the organism. As Dewey and Bentley,[13] Angyal,[14] Brunswik,[15] and many others have suggested, organism/environment is a unified pattern of behavior somewhat like a field in physics — not an interaction but a transaction. As Gardner Murphy has put it:

> We cannot define the situation operationally except in relation to the specific organism which is involved; we cannot define the organism operationally...except in reference to the situation. Each serves to define the other.[16]

To define operationally is to say what happens, to describe behavior, and as soon as we do this we find that we are talking about transactions. We cannot describe movements without describing the area or space in which they occur; we would not know that a given star or galaxy was moving except by comparing its position with others around it. Likewise, when we describe the world as completely as we can, we find that we are describing the form of man, for the scientific description of the world is actually a description of experiments, of what *men do* when they investigate the world. Conversely, when we describe the form of man as completely as we can — his physical structure as well as his behavior in speech and action — we find that we are describing the world. There is no way of separating them except by not looking too carefully, that is, by ignorance.

The human behavior that we call perception, thought, speech, and action is a consistency of organism and environment of the same kind as eating. What happens when we touch and feel a rock? Speaking very crudely, the rock comes in touch with a multitude of nerve ends in our fingers, and any nerve in the whole pattern of ends which touches the rock "lights up." Imagine an enormous grid of electric lightbulbs connected with a tightly packed grid of push buttons. If I open my hand and with its whole surface push down a group of buttons, the bulbs will light up in a pattern approximately resembling my hand. The shape of the hand is "translated" into the pattern of buttons and bulbs. Similarly, the feeling of a rock is what happens in the "grid" of the nervous system when it translates a contact with the rock. But we have at our disposal "grids" far more complex than this — not only optical and auditory but also linguistic and mathematical. These, too, are patterns into whose terms the world is translated in the same way as the rock is translated into nerve patterns. Such a grid, for example, is the system of coordinates, three of space and one of time, in which we feel that the world is happening even though there are no actual lines of height, width, and depth filling all space, and though the earth does not go *ticktock* when it revolves. Such a grid is also the whole system of classes, or verbal pigeonholes, into which we sort the world as things or events; still or moving; light or dark; animal, vegetable, or mineral; bird, beast, or flower; past, present, or future.

It is obvious, then, that when we are talking about the order and structure of the world, we are talking about the order of our grids. "Laws, like the law of causation, etc., treat of the network and not of what the network describes."[17] In other words, what we call the regularities of nature are the regularities of our grids. For regularity cannot be noticed except by comparing one process with another — e.g., the rotation of the earth about the sun with the strictly measured rotation of the clock. (The clock, with its evenly spaced seconds and minutes, is here the grid.) In the same way, what appear to be necessities of nature as a whole may be no more than necessities of grammar or mathematics. When anyone says that an unsupported body which is heavier than air *necessarily* falls to the ground, the necessity is not in nature but in the rules of definition. If it did not fall to the ground, it would not fit what we mean by "heavier than air." Consider the way in which a great deal of mathematical thinking is actually done. The mathematician does not ask whether his constructions are applicable, whether they correspond to any constructions in the natural world. He simply goes ahead and *invents* mathematical forms, asking only that they be consistent with themselves, with their own postulates. But every now and then it subsequently turns out that these forms can be correlated, like clocks, with other natural processes.

The puzzling thing is that some of the "grids" which we invent work, and some do not. In the same way, some animal behaviors seem to fit the environment and some do not. Those of ants, for example, have remained stable for millions of years, but the huge fangs of the saber-toothed tiger, the vast bulk of the Sauria, and the great nose horns of the Titanotheriidae were experimental failures. It would perhaps be more exact to say that they worked for a while, but not for as long as the experiments of other species. But what seems to happen in most of these cases is that the organism/environment relationship "splits": the organism's attack upon or defense against the environment becomes too strong, so isolating it from its source of life. Or it may be that the organism is too conservative for a swiftly changing environment, which is really the same situation: the pattern is too rigid, too insistent on survival, and thus again isolated. Or it may be that the organism, considered as a field in itself, is in self-contradiction: the weight of the nose horn is too much for the muscles. Turning to the human species, we may wonder whether such a split is taking place in the development of the overisolated consciousness of the individual.

If this be so, we must be careful of a false step in reasoning.

We must not say to the individual, "Watch out! If you want to survive you must *do* something about it!" Any action along these lines will simply make things worse; it will simply confirm the individual in his feeling of separation. It will become, like the nose horn, a survival mechanism frustrating survival. But if it is not up to the individual to do something, what is there to be said or done, and to whom and by whom?

Is it entirely unreasonable to suppose that the situation may correct itself, that the "field pattern" man/universe may be intelligent enough to do so? If this happens, or is happening, it will at first appear that individuals are initiating the changes on their own. But as the required change takes place, the individuals involved will simultaneously undergo a change of consciousness revealing the illusion of their isolation. May not something of the same kind be happening when a research worker, thinking that he has made an independent discovery, learns to his astonishment that several other people hit upon it at about the same time? As scientists sometimes say, the *field* of research had developed to the point where this particular discovery might naturally break out at several places.*

If we turn now to the social institution of language, or the "grid of words," we can easily see the ways in which it may be splitting organism from environment, and aspects of the environment from one another. Languages with such parts of speech as nouns and verbs obviously translate what is going on in the world into particular things (nouns) and events (verbs), and these in turn "have" properties (adjectives and adverbs) more or

---

* I, for example, as an "independent philosopher" could not possibly be saying what I am if I were really independent. "My" ideas are inseparable from what Northrop Frye calls "the order of words," i.e., the total pattern of literature and discourse now being unfolded throughout the world.

less separable from them. All such languages represent the world as if it were an assemblage of distinct bits and particles. The defect of such grids is that they screen out or ignore (or repress) interrelations. This is why it is so difficult to find the words to describe such fields as the organism/environment. Thus when the human body is analyzed and its organs are attached to nouns, we are at once in danger of the mechanical, overspecialized type of medicine and surgery which interferes at one point heedless of a disturbance of balance which may have unforeseen "effects" throughout the system. What *else* must the surgeon do if he has to remove a cancerous thyroid? Similar dangers arise in almost every sphere of human activity.

Let us suppose that social group A has an enemy, group B. The fact that B periodically attacks A keeps the members of A on their toes and "prunes" its population. But group A considers its own side good and B's side bad, and because good and bad are irreconcilable the actual service which B does for A is ignored. The time comes when A mobilizes its forces and either exterminates B or makes it incapable of further attack. A is then in danger of breeding itself out of existence, or of debilitation through lack of "tonus." An inadequate system of classification has made it too difficult to understand that there can be an enemy/friend and a war/collaboration. Obviously there is a similar relationship between virtue and vice. It has been pointed out so often, but society finds it too treasonable to take it seriously. As Lao-tzu said, "When everyone recognizes goodness to be good, there is already evil. Thus to be and not to be arise mutually."[18] It is that simple, but it just cannot be admitted! It is true that social action may get rid of such particular evils as judicial torture, child labor, or leprosy, but after a brief lapse of time the general feeling of being alive remains the same. In

other words, the freezing and the boiling of our emotions remain the same whether the scale lies between 0 and 100 centigrade
or 32 and 212 Fahrenheit. At the same time, a contest between
virtue and vice may remain as important as the contest between group A and group B. To see this, however, is to understand that the contest is a game.

All classification seems to require a division of the world. As
soon as there is a class, there is what is inside it and what is outside it. In and out, yes and no, are explicitly exclusive of one another. They are formally opposed, like group A and its enemy,
group B; good and bad; virtue and vice. The separation between
them seems to be as clear-cut as that between a solid and a space,
a figure and its background. The separation, the difference, is
therefore what we notice; it fits the notation of language, and because it is noted and explicit it is conscious and unrepressed. But
there is also something unnoticed and ignored, which does not
fit the notation of the language, and which because it is unnoted
and implicit is unconscious and repressed. This is that the inside
and the outside of the class go together and cannot do without
each other. "To be and not to be" arise mutually. Beneath the
contest lies friendship; beneath the serious lies the playful; beneath the separation of the individual and the world lies the field
pattern. In this pattern every push from within is at the same
time a pull from without, every explosion an implosion, every
outline an inline, arising mutually and simultaneously so that it
is always impossible to say from which side of a boundary any
movement begins. The individual no more acts *upon* the world
than the world upon the individual. The cause and the effect
turn out to be integral parts of the same event.

Wrestling as we are with languages whose forms resist
and screen out insights of this kind, it is understandable that at

present this view is only hypothetical in the behavioral sciences however well verified it may be in the physical. This is perhaps due in part to the fact that it is much easier to describe pure process and pattern in mathematics than in words, with their subjects, verbs, and predicates, their agents and acts. But we have not as yet gone very far in the mathematical description of living behavior. Yet it is not so hard to imagine a language which might describe all that man "is" and does as *doing*. After all, we can speak of a group of homes as housing without feeling impelled to ask, "*What* is it that is housing?" I do not think that such a language would be impoverished, any more than the sciences are impoverished through having given up such mysterious entities as the ether, the humors, phlogiston, and the planetary spheres. On the contrary, a language would be greatly enriched by making it easier for us to understand relationships which our present languages conceal. Described simply as pattern in motion, the mystery of what acts and what is acted upon, of how the cause issues in the effect, would be as easy as seeing the relationship between the concave and convex sides of a curve. Which side comes first?

The difficulty, however, is not so much in finding the language as in overcoming social resistance. Would it really do to find out that our game is not serious, that enemies are friends, and that the good thrives on the evil? Society as we know it seems to be a tacit conspiracy to keep this hushed up for fear that the contest will otherwise cease. If these opposites are not kept fiercely separate and antagonistic, what motivation will there be for the creative struggle between them? If man does not feel himself at war with nature, will there be any further impetus to technological progress? Imagine how the Christian conscience would react to the idea that, behind the scenes, God and the Devil were the closest friends but had taken opposite sides in order to stage a great cosmic game. Yet this is rather much how things stood when the Book of Job was written, for here Satan is simply the counsel for the prosecution in the court of Heaven, as faithful a servant of the court as the *advocatus diaboli* at the Vatican.*

The problem is, of course, that if men are patterns of action and not agents, and if the individual and the world act with each other, mutually, so that action does not originate in either, who is to be blamed when things go wrong? Can the police then come around asking, "Who started this?" The convention of the individual as the responsible, independent agent is basic to almost all our social and legal structures. Acceptance of this role or identity is the chief criterion of sanity, and we feel that if anyone is reducible to actions or behaviors with nobody doing them, he must be no more than a soulless mechanism. Indeed, there is at first glimpse an element of terror in this universe of pure activity; there seems to be no point from which to make a decision, to begin anything. It is not at all unlikely that some kind of slip into this way of feeling things may sometimes touch off a psychotic break, for the individual might well feel that he had lost control of everything and could no longer trust himself or others to behave consistently. But supposing one understood in the first place that this is the way things are anyhow, the experience itself would be far less unnerving. In practice it happens that just as soon as one gets used to this feeling and is not afraid of it, it is possible to go on behaving as rationally as ever — but with a remarkable sense of lightness.

Setting aside, for the time being, the moral and ethical

---

* I find it, likewise, difficult to read the stories of the Last Supper without getting the impression that Jesus *commanded* Judas to betray him.

implications of this view of man, it seems to have the same sort of advantage over the ordinary view that the Copernican solar system has over the Ptolemaic. It is so much simpler, even though it means giving up the central position of the earth. This is, moreover, the kind of simplicity which is fruitful rather than diminishing: it leads to further possibilities of play, greater richness of articulation. On the other hand, the ordinary conventional view seems increasingly to fail in what it purports to achieve.

One of the best accounts of the social and conventional character of the ego is in the work of George Herbert Mead.[19] He points out that the difference between the social and the biological theories of the origin of individual self-consciousness corresponds to the difference between evolutionary and contract theories of the origin of the state. In the latter, discredited view the social community is formed by deliberate contract between self-conscious persons. He reasons, however, that the individual cannot become an object to himself by himself, and in any case no animate individuals have ever existed by themselves.

> The view that mind [i.e., the ego] is a congenital biological endowment of the individual organism does not really enable us to explain its nature and origin at all: neither what sort of biological endowment it is, nor how organisms at a certain level of evolutionary progress come to possess it.[20]

He goes on to show that the "I," the biological individual, can become conscious of itself only in terms of the "me," but that this latter is a view of itself given to it by other people.

> The individual enters as such into his own experience only as an object, not as a subject; and he can enter as an object only on the basis of social relations and interactions, only by means of his experiential transactions with other

individuals in an organized social environment...only by
taking the attitudes of others towards himself — is he able
to become an object to himself.[21]

As a result the mind, or psychological structure of the individual, cannot be identified with some entity inside his skin.

> If mind is socially constituted, then the field or locus of
> any given individual mind must extend as far as the social
> activity or apparatus of social relations which constitutes
> it extends; and hence that field cannot be bounded by the
> skin of the individual organism to which it belongs.[22]

And that is just the paradox of the situation: society gives us the
idea that the mind, or ego,* is inside the skin and that it acts on its
own apart from society.

Here, then, is a major contradiction in the rules of the social
game. The members of the game are to play *as if* they were independent agents, but they are not to *know* that they are just
playing as if! It is explicit in the rules that the individual is self-
determining, but implicit that he is so only by virtue of the rules.
Furthermore, while he is defined as an independent agent, he
must not be so independent as not to submit to the rules which
define him. Thus he is defined as an agent in order to be held
responsible to the group for "his" actions. The rules of the game
confer independence and take it away at the same time, without
revealing the contradiction.

This is exactly the predicament which Gregory Bateson[23]

---

* Mead himself does not use the term "ego" in quite this sense, for he associates
  it with the "I" rather than with the "me." But since he is also associating the "I"
  with the organism, this seems quite inconsistent, for the ego is almost invariably
  considered as something *in* the organism, like the chauffeur in a car, or a little man
  inside the head who thinks thoughts and sees sights. It is just this ego feeling that
  is the social construct.

calls the "double-bind," in which the individual is called upon to take two mutually exclusive courses of action and at the same time is prevented from being able to comment on the paradox. You are damned if you do and damned if you don't, and you mustn't realize it. Bateson has suggested that the individual who finds himself in a family situation which imposes the double-bind upon him in an acute form is liable to schizophrenia.* For if he cannot comment on the contradiction, what can he do but withdraw from the field? Yet society does not allow withdrawal; the individual *must* play the game. As Thoreau said, wherever you may seek solitude men will ferret you out "and compel you to belong to their desperate company of oddfellows." Thus in order to withdraw, the individual must imply that *he* is not withdrawing, that his withdrawal is happening, and that he cannot help himself. In other words, he must "lose his mind" and become insane.

But as "genius is to madness close allied," the schizophrenic withdrawal is a caricature of liberation, including even the "lamasery" of the insane asylum or the peculiarly exempt status of the old-fashioned village idiot. As the terminology of Zen Buddhism implies, the liberated man also has "no mind" (*wu-hsin*) and does not feel himself to be an agent, a doer of deeds. So also it is said in the *Bhagavadgita*:

> The man who is united with the Divine and knows the
> truth thinks "I do nothing at all," for in seeing, hearing,
> touching, smelling, tasting, walking, sleeping, breathing;

---

* While he has assembled a good deal of evidence in support of this suggestion, he does not claim to have proved it. Other research is suggesting that schizophrenia may be explained chemically as a toxic condition, but the two points of view do not necessarily exclude each other. The stress induced by the double-bind situation could have something to do with generating the toxin.

in speaking, emitting, grasping, opening and closing the eyes he holds that only the senses are occupied with the objects of the senses.[24]

But in liberation this comes to pass not through an unconscious compulsion but through insight, through understanding and breaking the double-bind which society imposes. One does not then get into the position of not being able to play the game; one can play it all the better for seeing that it is a game.

The schizophrenic withdrawal affects a minority, and it occurs in circumstances in which the double-bind imposed by society in general is compounded by special types of double-bind peculiar to a special family situation.* The rest of us are in differing degrees of neurosis, tolerable to the extent to which we can forget the contradiction thrust upon us, to which we can "forget ourselves" by absorption in hobbies, mystery novels, social service, television, business, and warfare. Thus it is hard to avoid the conclusion that we are accepting a definition of sanity which is insane, and that as a result our common human problems are so persistently insoluble that they add up to the perennial and universal "predicament of man," which is attributed to nature, to the Devil, or to God himself.

If what has been said up to this point is intelligible, it is only partly so; otherwise the reader would have been liberated forthwith! As I have suggested, there are unavoidable verbal difficulties even in describing the paradox we are in, let alone in describing the actual field pattern in which human life takes place. The trouble is that we are describing the difficulty with the very language structure that gets us into it. It has to say, "*We* are

---

* As when a mother requires her child to love her and yet withdraws from expressions of affection.

describing" and "Gets *us* into it," confirming at every step the reality of the agent-entity presumed to stand behind the activity, or to be enduring it when it is understood to be coming from some other source. Common sense balks at the notion of action without agent just as it balks at the idea of pattern without substance, whether material or mental. But $1 + 2 = 3$ and $x - y = z$ are intelligible statements of relation without our having to ask what any of the symbols stand for, whether things or events, solids or spaces.

Thus the whole difficulty of both psychotherapy and liberation is that the problems which they address lie in the social institutions in whose terms we think and act. No cooperation can be expected from an individual ego which is itself the social institution at the root of the trouble. But these institutions are observable; we do not have to ask, "By whom?" They are observable *here*, for, as William James pointed out, "The word 'I'...is primarily a noun of position like 'this' and 'here.'"[25] If they are observable they are subject to comment, and it is the ability to comment upon it that breaks the double-bind. On the one hand, social institutions like the grid of language create, or better, translate, the world in their terms, so that the world — life itself — appears to be self-contradictory if the terms are self-contradictory. On the other hand, social institutions do not create the world *ex nihilo*. They are in and of the pattern of nature which they in turn represent or misrepresent.

The pattern of nature can be *stated* only in terms of a language; but it can be *shown* in terms of, say, sense perceptions. For a society whose number system is only "1, 2, 3, many," it cannot be a fact that we have ten fingers, and yet all the fingers are visible. People who *know*, for whom it is a fact, that they are egos or that the sun goes around the earth can be shown that their facts are wrong by being persuaded to act consistently upon them. If you know that the earth is flat, sail consistently in one direction until you fall off the edge. Similarly, if you know that you are an independent agent, do something quite independently, be deliberately spontaneous, and show me this agent.

That there is a pattern of nature can be shown; *what* it is can be stated, and we can never be certain that what we have stated is finally correct because there is nothing about which we can act consistently *forever*. But when we are employing institutions in whose terms we cannot act consistently, we may be sure either that they are self-contradictory or that they do not fit the pattern of nature. Self-contradictions which are not observed and patterns of nature which the language screens out are, in psychological terms, unconscious and repressed. Social institutions are then in conflict with the actual pattern of the man-in-the-world, and this comes out as distress in the individual organism, which *cannot* be inconsistent with itself or with nature without ceasing to exist. Freud was therefore right as far as he went in tracing neurosis to the conflict between sexual feeling and the peculiar sexual mores of Western cultures. But he was only scratching the surface. For one thing, his view of the sexual "instinct" itself was heavily conditioned by those very mores. As Philip Rieff has said:

> Not only did Freud employ sexuality to deflate the pride of civilized man, he further defined it pejoratively by those qualities which make the sexual instinct intractable to a civilized sensibility.... While urging, for the sake of our mental health, that we dispense with such childish fantasies of purity as are epitomized in the belief that Mother (or Father) was too nice to have done those nasty things,

> Freud at the same time comes to the tacit understanding
> that sex really is nasty, an ignoble slavery to nature.[26]

For another, Freud's interpretation of the id and its libido as blind and brutish urges was simply a reflection of the current philosophy that the world is basically "mere" energy, a sort of crude volatile stuff, rather than organic pattern — which is, after all, another name for intelligence.

But what our social institutions repress is not just the sexual love, the mutuality, of man and woman, but also the still deeper love of organism and environment, of Yes and No, and of all those so-called opposites represented in the Taoist symbol of the *yang-yin*, the black and white fishes in eternal intercourse. It is hardly stretching a metaphor to use the word "love" for intimate relationships beyond those between human organisms. In those states of consciousness called "mystical" we have, I believe, a sudden slip into an inverse or obverse of the view of the world given in our divisive language forms. Where this slip is not, as in schizophrenia, a tortured withdrawal from conflict, the change of consciousness again and again brings the overwhelming impression that the world is a system of love. Everything fits into place in an indescribable harmony — indescribable because paradoxical in the terms which our language provides.

Now our language forms, our grids of thought, are by no means wholly wrong. The differences and divisions in the world which they note are surely there to be seen. There are indeed some mere ghosts of language, but in the main the categories of language seem to be valid and indeed essential to any description of the world whatsoever — as far as they go. But a given language cannot properly express what is implicit in it — the unity of differences, the logical inseparability of light and darkness, Yes and No. The question is whether these logical implications

correspond to physical relations. The whole trend of modern
science seems to be establishing the fact that, for the most part,
they do. Things must be seen together with the form of the space
between them. As Ernst Cassirer said as long ago as 1923:

> The new physical view proceeds neither from the assump-
> tion of a "space in itself," nor of "matter" nor of "force in
> itself " — it no longer recognizes space, force and matter
> as physical objects separated from each other, but...only
> the unity of certain *functional relations*, which are differ-
> ently designated according to the system of reference in
> which we express them.[27]

While we must be careful not to overstress analogies between
physics and human behavior, there must certainly be general
principles in common between them. Compare what Cassirer
said with Gardner Murphy:

> I have believed for a long time that human nature is a rec-
> iprocity of what is inside the skin and what is outside; that
> it is definitely not "rolled up inside us" but our way of
> being one with our fellows and our world. I call this field
> theory.[28]

The ways of liberation are of course concerned with making this so-called mystical consciousness the normal everyday
consciousness. But I am more and more persuaded that what
happens in their disciplines, regardless of the language in which
it is described, is nothing either supernatural or metaphysical in
the usual sense. It has nothing to do with a perception of something else than the physical world. On the contrary, it is the clear
perception of this world as a field, a perception which is not just
theoretical but which is also felt as clearly as we feel, say, that
"I" am a thinker behind and apart from my thoughts, or that the

stars are absolutely separate from space and from each other. In this view the differences of the world are not isolated objects encountering one another in conflict, but expressions of polarity. Opposites and differences have something between them, like the two faces of a coin; they do not meet as total strangers. When this relativity of things is seen very strongly, its appropriate affect is love rather than hate or fear.

Surely this is the way of seeing things that is required for effective psychotherapy. Disturbed individuals are, as it were, points in the social field where contradictions in the field break out. It will not do at all to confirm the contradictions from which they are suffering, for the psychiatrist to be the official representative of a sick system of institutions. The society of men with men and the larger ecological society of men with nature, however explicitly a contest, is implicitly a field — an agreement, a relativity, a game. The rules of the game are conventions, which again mean agreements. It is fine for us to agree that we are different from each other, provided we do not ignore the fact that we *agreed* to differ. We did not differ to agree, to create society by deliberate contract between originally independent parties. Furthermore, even if there is to be a battle, there must be a field of battle; when the contestants really notice this they will have a war dance instead of a war.

III. The Ways of Liberation

If it is true that psychotherapy has not been seen clearly in its social context, it is also true of the Eastern ways of liberation as they have been studied and explained in the West. Almost all the modern literature on Buddhism, Vedanta, and Taoism treats these subjects in a void with the barest minimum of reference to the larger background of Indian or Chinese culture. One gathers, therefore, that these disciplines are exportable units like bales of rice or tea, and that Buddhism can be "taken up" anywhere at any time like baseball. It has also seemed to the West that Christianity can be exported in the same way, that it will "work" in any culture, and, if not, so much the worse for that culture. At the same time let it be said that, at least in the higher civilizations, there are no such things as "pure" cultures uncontaminated by exotic influences. Buddhism did in fact travel from India to the very different cultures of China, Tibet, Thailand, and Japan in a way that Hinduism, as a total culture, could never

have traveled. But wherever there was not some parallel institution, such as Taoism in China, it was difficult to assimilate and
understand. In other words, it becomes intelligible — and applicable in our own terms — when we can see its relation to the
culture from which it comes. In this way we can borrow things
from other cultures, but always only to the extent that they suit
our own needs.

One of the blessings of easy communication between the
great cultures of the world is that partisanship in religion or
philosophy is ceasing to be intellectually respectable. Pure religions are as rare as pure cultures, and it is mentally crippling to
suppose that there must be a number of fixed bodies of doctrine
among which one must choose, where choice means accepting
the system entirely or not at all. Highly organized religions always try to force such a choice because they need devoted members for their continuance. Those who rove freely through the
various traditions, accepting what they can use and rejecting
what they cannot, are condemned as undisciplined syncretists.
But the use of one's reason is not a lack of discipline, nor is there
any important religion which is not itself a syncretism, a "growing up together" of ideas and practices of diverse origin. Time
will indeed give any religious syncretism an organic unity of
its own, but also a rigidity which needs to be shaken. But one
of the consequences of taking Buddhism or Vedanta out of its
own cultural context is, as we have seen, the supposition that it
is a religion in the same sense as Christianity and with the same
social function.

Thus it strikes the uninformed Westerner that Buddhism
could be an alternative to Christianity: a body of metaphysical, cosmological, psychological, and moral doctrine to be believed and simply substituted for what one has believed before.

It also seems that the actual practice of these ways of liberation is almost entirely a matter of one's private life. They seem to be solitary explorations of man's inner consciousness, presumed to be the same everywhere, and thus as applicable in California as in Bengal — the more so because they do not require membership in a church. Yet if the main function of a way of liberation is to release the individual from his "hypnosis" by certain social institutions, what is needed in California will not be quite the same as what is needed in Bengal, for the institutions differ. Like different diseases, they require different medicines.

Yet very few modern authorities on Buddhism or Vedanta seem to realize that social institutions constitute the *maya*, the illusion, from which they offer release. It is almost invariably assumed that *Nirvana* or *moksha* means release from the physical organism and the physical universe, an accomplishment involving powers of mind over matter that would give their possessor the omnipotence of a god. Aside, however, from some competent extrasensory perception and some imaginative use of hypnosis, no such powers have been demonstrated, though we shall have more to say about the therapeutic use of trickery.* Some discussions of liberation suggest that what is involved is not so much objective as subjective release from the physical world. In other words, it is assumed that our normal perception of the spatially and temporally extended world, and of the sense organs which transact with it, is a type of hypnotic illusion, and that anyone who acquires perfect concentration can see for himself that the spatiotemporal world is nothing but imagination. From

---

* To some this may seem a bold statement, but it has always struck me as important that demonstrations of occult powers are almost invariably trivial in their achievements, e.g., cracking teacups at a distance, causing vases to fall off shelves, and alleged teleportations of small objects.

what we know of the hypnotic state and its induction by concentration, it might be easy enough to produce the impression
that this is so. If the operator can make himself invisible to the
subject, why cannot he make the whole universe invisible? But I
do not believe that the ways of liberation amount to anything so
trivial as substituting one hypnotic state for another. We know
that our perception of the world is relative to our neurological
structure and the ways in which social conditioning has taught
us to see. Because the latter can to some extent be changed, it
means something to say that it is imaginary. But is the structure
of the organism imaginary? No one can prove that it is unless he
can demonstrate that it can change itself radically by other than
surgical means.

All my experience of those who are proficient in the ways
of liberation indicates that feats of magic or neurotechnology
are quite beside the point. I have known one Zen master quite
intimately, as a personal friend, and have met and talked with
many others, as well as a considerable number of yogis and swa-
mis both honest and phony. Furthermore, I have reliable friends
who have studied and practiced with Zen and Yoga teachers far
more extensively than I, and I have found no evidence whatsoever for any sensational achievements of this kind. If they have
achieved anything at all it is of a far humbler nature and in quite
a different direction, and something which strikes me as actually
more impressive.

It is not within the scope of this book to present a fully doc-
umented argument for the idea that liberation is from the *maya*
of social institutions and not of the physical world. Some evidence will be given, but I have not myself arrived at this idea by
a rigorous examination of documents. It is simply a hypothesis
which, to me, makes far better sense of Buddhism and Vedanta,

Yoga and Taoism, than any other interpretation. The documents are often ambiguous, for what we mean by the real or physical world is obviously determined by social institutions. When Buddhist texts state that all things (*dharma*) are falsely imagined and without reality of their own (*svabhava*) this can mean (a) that the concrete physical universe does not exist, or (b) that things are relative: they have no self-existence because no one thing can be designated without relation to others, and furthermore because "thing" is a unit of description — not a natural entity. If the former interpretation is correct, the Buddhist *Nirvana* will be an utterly blank state of consciousness; if the latter, it will be a transformed view of the physical world, seeing that world in its full relativity. Can there be any reasonable doubt that the latter is intended?*

If, then, the *maya* or unreality lies not in the physical world but in the concepts or thought forms by which it is described, it is clear that *maya* refers to social institutions — to language and logic and their constructs — and to the way in which they modify our feeling of the world. This becomes even clearer when

---

* Buddhism is of course a matrix of many different schools with formally divergent points of view, and in their strictly popular forms some of these schools are certainly religions and not ways of liberation. When, therefore, I use the word "Buddhism" without further qualification it should be understood that I am referring to the Madhyamika school of Nagarjuna, described by T. R. V. Murti[29] as the central philosophy of Buddhism. With regard to the reality of the world, Murti writes: "The Absolute is not one reality set against another, the empirical. The Absolute looked at through thought-forms (vikalpa) is phenomenon (samsara or samvrta, literally covered). The latter, freed of the superimposed thought-forms (nirvikalpa, nisprapanca), is the Absolute. The difference is epistemic (subjective), and not ontological. Nagarjuna therefore declares that there is not the least difference between the world and the absolutely real. Transcendent to thought, the Absolute, however, is thoroughly immanent in experience." Cf. Wittgenstein, "Not *how* the world is, is the mystical, but *that* it is. . . . There is indeed the inexpressible. This *shows* itself; it is the mystical."[30]

we look at the relation of the Indian ways of liberation to the social structure and popular cosmology of the ancient Aryan culture. The community is divided into four basic castes — Brahman (priestly), Kshatriya (military), Vaishya (mercantile), and Sudra (laboring) — in terms of which the role and identity of every individual is defined. An individual outside caste has no legal identity, and is thus regarded as a human animal rather than a human person. The four castes are, furthermore, the general classification of roles temporarily assumed by something beyond man and, indeed, beyond all classification. This is the Brahman, or Godhead, which is one and the same as the Atman, the essential Self playing each individual role. In this ancient Indian cosmology the creation of the world is thus a dramatic manifestation. The Godhead is playing at being finite; the One is pretending to be many, but in the process, in assuming each individual role, the One has, so to speak, forgotten Itself and so has become involved in unconsciousness or ignorance (*avidya*).

So long as this ignorance prevails, the individualized form of the Godhead, the soul or *jivatman*, is constantly reborn into the world, rising or falling in fortune and station according to its deeds and their consequences (*karma*). There are various levels above and below the human through which the individual soul may pass in the course of its reincarnations — the angelic, the titanic, the animal, the purgatories, and the realm of frustrated ghosts. Until it awakens to full self-knowledge, the individual soul may undergo reincarnation for amazingly long periods of time, touching the highest possibilities of pleasure and the lowest depths of pain, going round and round upon the wheel of *samsara* for thousands and millions of years.

If we go back in imagination to an India entirely uninfluenced by Western ideas, and especially those of Western science, it is easy to see that this cosmology would have been something much more than a belief. It would have seemed to be a matter of fact which everyone *knew* to be true. It was taken for granted, and was also vouched for by the authority of the most learned men of the time, an authority just as impressive then as scientific authority is today. Without the distraction of some persuasive alternative one can know that such a cosmology is true just as one can know that the sun goes around the earth — or just as one can know that the following figure is a bear climbing a tree, without being able to see the bear:

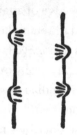

Or is it simply a trunk with burls on it?

To the degree, then, that this cosmology was a matter of ingrained common sense, it would have been as difficult for the average Hindu to see the world otherwise as it is for us to imagine what a physicist means by curved space, or to believe him when he says that matter is not solid.

All the ways of liberation offered release from the endless cycle of reincarnation — Vedanta and Yoga through the awakening of the true Self, and Buddhism through the realization that the process of life is not happening to any subject, so that there no longer remains anyone to be reincarnated. They agreed, in other words, that the individual soul with its continued reincarnation from life to life and even from moment to moment is *maya*, a playful illusion. Yet all popular accounts of these doctrines, both

Western and Asian, state that so long as the individual remains unliberated he will in fact continue to be reincarnated. Despite the Buddhist *anatman* doctrine of the unreality of the substantial ego, the *Milindapanha* records Nagasena's complex efforts to convince the Greek king Menander that reincarnation can occur, without any actual soul, until at last *Nirvana* is attained. The vast majority of Asian Hindus and Buddhists continue to believe that reincarnation is a fact, and most Westerners adopting Vedanta or Buddhism adopt belief in reincarnation at the same time. Western Buddhists even find this belief consoling, in flat contradiction to the avowed objective of attaining release from rebirth.

It is, however, logical to retain the belief in reincarnation as a fact if one also believes that *maya* is the physical world as distinct from ideas *about* the physical world. That is to say, one will continue to believe in this Indian cosmology until one realizes that it is a social institution. I wish, therefore, to commend what to many students of these doctrines may seem to be a startling thesis: that Buddhists and Vedantists who understand their own doctrines profoundly, who are in fact liberated, do not believe in reincarnation in any liberal sense. Their liberation involved, among other things, the realization that the Hindu cosmology was a myth and not a fact. It was, and remains, a liberation from being taken in by social institutions; it is not liberation from being alive. It is consistent with this view that, in India, liberation went hand in hand with renunciation of caste; the individual ceased to identify himself with his socially defined identity, his role. He underlined this ritually by abandoning family responsibilities when his sons were able to assume them, by discarding clothes, or, as in the case of the Buddhists, by donning the ocher robes which marked the criminal outcaste, and by retiring to the forests and mountains. Mahayana Buddhism later introduced the final and logical refinement — the bodhisattva who returns to society and adopts its conventions without "attachment," who in other words *plays* the social game instead of taking it seriously.

If this thesis is true, why was it not stated openly, and why have the majority of Buddhists and Vedantists been allowed to go on thinking of the reincarnation cosmology as fact? There are two reasons. First, liberation is not revolution. It is not going out of one's way to disturb the social order by casting doubt upon the conventional ideas by which people hold together. Furthermore, society is always insecure and thus hostile to any-one who challenges its conventions directly. To disabuse oneself of accepted mythologies without becoming the victim of other people's anxiety requires considerable tact. Second, the whole technique of liberation requires that the individual shall find out the truth for himself. Simply to tell it is not convincing. In-stead, he must be asked to experiment, to act consistently upon assumptions which he holds to be true until he finds out other-wise. The *guru* or teacher of liberation must therefore use all his skill to persuade the student to act upon his own delusions, for the latter will always resist any undermining of the props of his security. He teaches not by explanation, but by pointing out new ways of acting upon the student's false assumptions until the student convinces himself that they are false.

Herein, I feel, is the proper explanation of the esotericism of the ways of liberation. The initiate is one who knows that cer-tain social institutions are self-contradictory or in actual conflict with the form of nature. But he knows also that these institutions have the strongest emotions invested in them. They are the rules of communication whereby people understand one another, and they have been beaten into the behavior patterns of impres-sionable children with the full force social anxiety. At the same time, those who are taken in by such institutions are suffering from them — suffering from the very ideas which they believe to be vital to sanity and survival. There is therefore no way of disabusing the sufferer directly, by telling him that his cherished disease is a disease. If he is to be helped at all, he must be *tricked* into insight. If I am to help someone else to see that a false problem is false, I must pretend that I am taking his problem seriously. What I am actually taking seriously is his suffering, but he must be led to believe that it is what he considers as his problem.

Such trickery is basic to medicine and psychotherapy alike. It has been said that the good doctor is one who keeps the patient amused while nature works the cure. This is not always true, but it is a sound general principle. It is easier to wait for a natural change when one is given the impression that something is being done to bring it about. What is being done is the trick; the relaxed and rested waiting is the actual cure, but the anxiety which attends a disease makes direct and deliberate relaxation almost impossible. Patients lose confidence in their doctors to the extent that the trickery is exposed, and therefore the art of medicine progresses by the invention of new and ever more impenetrable tricks.

Let us suppose, then, that someone who is suffering from a social institution imagines that he is suffering because of an actual conflict in life, in the very structure of the physical world — that nature threatens his presumably physical ego. The healer must then appear to be a magician, a master of the physical world. He must do whatever is necessary to convince the sufferer that he can solve what seems to the latter to be a physical problem, for there is no other way of convincing him to do what is necessary for acting consistently upon his false assumption.

He must above all convince the sufferer that he, the *guru*, has
mastered the imaginary problem, that *his* ego is not disturbed
by pain or death or worldly passions. Moreover, because the disease was engendered by social authority, the *guru* must appear to
have equal or superior social authority to the parents, relatives,
and instructors of the patient. In all this the Eastern ways of liberation have been astonishingly ingenious; their masters, whom
society would have felt to be utterly subversive, have convinced
society that they are its very pillars. It is thus that the *guru* who
has a bad temper or who likes to smoke or drink sake gives the
impression that he indulges in these "little vices" deliberately
in order to remain in his bodily manifestation, for if he were
consistently unattached to the physical world he would cease to
appear in it.

Stated thus baldly the technique will naturally seem to be
dishonest. But this is a conscious and deliberate dishonesty
to counter an unconscious and otherwise ineradicable self-
deception on the homeopathic principle of *similia similibus cu-
rantur* — likes are cured by likes. Set a thief to catch a thief.
Speaking of mutual recognition between those who are liberated, a Zen Buddhist text says:

> *When two thieves meet they need no introduction:*
> *They recognize each other without question.*[31]

Of course the *guru* is human like everyone else. His advantage,
his liberation, lies in the fact that he is not in conflict with himself
for being so; he is not in the double-bind of pretending that he
is an independent agent without knowing that he is pretending,
of imagining that he is an ego or subject which can somehow
manage to be permanently "one up" on its correlative object

— the changing panorama of experiences, sensations, feelings, emotions, and thoughts. The *guru* accepts himself; more exactly, he does not think of himself as something other than his behavior patterns, as something which performs them. On the other hand, social conditioning as we know it depends entirely on persuading people *not* to accept themselves, and necessary as this stratagem, this "as if," may be for training the young, it is a fiction of limited use. The more it succeeds, the more it fails. Civilization attained at the price of inculcating this fiction permanently is necessarily self-destructive, and by comparison with such disaster the *guru*'s "dishonesty" is a positive virtue.

A Japanese coastal village was once threatened by a tidal wave, but the wave was sighted in advance, far out on the horizon, by a lone farmer in the rice fields on the hillside above the village. At once he set fire to the fields, and the villagers who came swarming up to save their crops were saved from the flood. His crime of arson is like the trickery of the *guru*, the doctor, or the psychotherapist in persuading people to try to solve a false problem by acting consistently upon its premises.

This apparently unorthodox account of the basic method of the ways of liberation is required, I feel, to explain a number of problems. However various their doctrines and however different their formal techniques, all seem to culminate in the same state or mode of consciousness in which the duality of the ego and the world is overcome. Call it "cosmic consciousness" or "mystical experience," or what you will, it seems to me to be the felt realization of the physical world as a field. But because language is divisive rather than relational, not only is the feeling hard to describe but also our attempted descriptions may seem to be opposed. Buddhism emphasizes the unreality of the ego, whereas Vedanta emphasizes the unity of the field. Thus in describing liberation the former seems to be saying simply that the egocentric viewpoint evaporates, and the latter, that we discover our true self to be the Self of the universe. However pundits may argue the fine points, it comes to the same thing in practical experience.

There is, then, nothing occult or supernatural in this state of consciousness, and yet the traditional methods for attaining it are complex, divergent, obscure, and, for the most part extremely arduous. Confronted with such a tangle, one asks what is common to these methods, what is their essential ingredient; and if this can be found the result will be a practical and theoretical simplification of the whole problem. To do this we must look for a simplified and yet adequate way of describing what happens between the *guru* or Zen master and his student within the social context of their transaction. What we find is something very like a contest in judo: the expert does not attack; he waits for the attack, he lets the student pose the problem. Then, when the attack comes, he does not oppose it; he rolls with it and carries it to its logical conclusion, which is the downfall of the false social premise of the student's question.

Admittedly there may be many *gurus* who do not fully realize that this is what they are doing, just as there are many physicians who do not realize that some of their medications are placebos. Successful psychotherapy is carried out by Freudian psychoanalysis, by Rogers's nondirective counseling, and by Jung's analytical psychology. The theories and methods differ and diverge, but there may be some hidden and essential factor in common. Yet there is good reason to believe that some teachers of the ways of liberation know perfectly well what they are doing, that they are fully aware of their merciful trickery and

also of the fact that the release attained is not from physical reincarnation but from confused thinking and feeling.

Some evidence for this point of view must, however, be
presented if we are to be sure that psychotherapy and the ways
of liberation have common ground. We must start from the
well-recognized fact that all the ways of liberation, Buddhism,
Vedanta, Yoga, and Taoism,* assert that our ordinary egocentric consciousness is a limited and impoverished consciousness
without foundation in "reality." Whether its basis is physical
or social, biological or cultural, remains to be seen, but there is
no doubt that release from this particular limitation is the aim
of all four ways. In every case the method involves meditation,
which may take the form of concentrated attention upon some
particular object, problem, or aspect of consciousness, or simply of the relaxed and detached observation of whatever comes
into mind. It may take the form of trying to suppress all verbal
thinking, or the form of a dialectic in which the most rigorous
thinking is carried to its full conclusions. It may be an attempt
to be directly aware of the perceiving self, or it may follow out
the idea that the self is not anything that can be known, not the
body, not the sensations, not the thoughts, not even consciousness. In some instances the student is simply asked to find out,
exhaustively and relentlessly, *why* he wants liberation, or *who* it
is that wants to be liberated. Methods vary not only among the
differing schools and teachers but also in accordance with the
needs and temperaments of their disciples.

Some schools insist that a *guru* who is himself liberated is
absolutely essential to the task; others say only that this makes

---

* Perhaps I should also include Islamic Sufism and aspects of Jainism, but these are
subjects which I have not studied to anything like the same extent.

things much easier, but that it is not impossible for the student to play the game upon himself. There is a similar division of opinion about psychotherapy. But in fact there is always a *guru* in some sense, even if it be only a friend who has given one the idea, or perhaps a book that one has read. The bondage that arises from a social relationship has to be released through social relationship. Both are functions of relationship — as is life itself.

Is it actually understood in Asia that liberation is from social rather than from physical or metaphysical conditions? My own questioning of Zen Buddhist teachers on this point leaves no doubt about it. I have not found one that believes in reincarnation as a physical fact, still less one who lays claims to any literally miraculous powers over the physical world. All such matters are understood symbolically. What about the mysterious "masters of Tibet" to whom so much has been attributed in the way of occult knowledge about the superphysical worlds? While there is much purely literary and scholastic information about the texts of Tibetan Buddhism, very few Westerners have actually practiced its disciplines on the spot. An exception is Madame Alexandra David-Neel, a remarkable Frenchwoman who has recently written an equally remarkable book to try to explain as much as possible of the fundamental doctrine of her teachers. She writes:

> If [the student] cannot refuse to play a role in the comedy or drama of the world, at least he understands that it is all a game.... They teach him to look...at the incessant working of his mind and the physical activity displayed by the body. He ought to succeed in understanding, in noting that nothing of all that is *from him*, is *him*. *He*, physically and mentally, is the multitude of others.

> This "multitude of others" includes the material elements — the ground, one might say — which he owes to his heredity, to his atavism, then those which he has ingested, which he has inhaled from before his birth, by the help of which his body was formed, and which, assimilated by him, have become with the complex forces inherent in them constituent parts of his being.
>
> On the mental plane, this "multitude of others" includes many beings who are his contemporaries: people he consorts with, with whom he chats, whose actions he watches. Thus a continual inhibition is at work while the individual absorbs a part of the various energies given off by those with whom he is in contact, and these incongruous energies, installing themselves in that which he considers his "I," form there a swarming throng.
>
> This actually includes a considerable number of beings belonging to what we call the Past....personalities with which he might have been in contact in the course of his reading and during his education.[32]

This is no other than a description of the organism, the body, as inseparable from a system of physical relations, and of the ego as G. H. Mead's "generalized other," the individual's feeling or conception of himself arising from social intercourse. As to reincarnation, she continues:

> When the student becomes aware of this crowd in himself, he should avoid imagining, as some do, that it represents memories of his preceding lives. There is no lack of those who state and are convinced that such and such a personage, who lived in the past, is reincarnated in them. Stories depicting reincarnations are innumerable in Asia

where they keep alive the childish thirst for the marvellous among the masses.[33]

In other words, reincarnation is not understood literally as the successive reembodiment of an individual ego, or even of an individual "chain of *karma*" or causally connected behavior pattern.* The individual's multitude of lives is interpreted as the multitude of his physical and social relations.

I do not wish to dwell tediously on the theme of understanding reincarnation symbolically rather than physically, but it is somewhat crucial for realizing that *maya* lies in the social sphere of description and thought, and not in the larger sphere of natural and physical relations. Something should, however, be said as to the Buddha's own attitude to the problem, insofar as it can be recovered. It is clear from the canonical texts that he denied the reality of any substantial ego, but that he neither denied nor affirmed the possibility of past or future "lives." He considered it irrelevant because he was concerned with man's liberation not from the physical world but from the egocentric

---

* The hypothesis of the individual chain of *karma* as distinct from the soul entity (*jivatman*) was invoked by Nagasena and many others to preserve physical and literal reincarnation as a Buddhist doctrine. But what *other* hypothesis does this require to account for connections between a *karma*-chain running from, say, 1600 to 1650 and the same chain's next incarnation between 1910 and 1975? Through what system of relations does the chain maintain its identity in the interim? I do not deny that such a system *may* exist. The point is only that whether it exists is irrelevant to a correct understanding of Buddhism. According to the Madhyamika philosophy of Nagarjuna, the linear, catenary causal chain between "things" is purely conceptual (*vikalpa*) and descriptive. Murti,[34] in trying too hard to assimilate the Madhyamika to Kantian ideas, makes the strange confusion of saying that Nagarjuna intended this critique of causality to apply to the noumenal world and not to the phenomenal. But which of these two is the physical? Surely both are the physical — but the phenomenal world, in which causality applies, is the physical world described *as phenomena*, as if it were separate things and events. But how much confusion could be avoided if it were kept clear that things, or phenomena, are units of description, not of what we are describing.

style of consciousness. Whether such liberation did or did not terminate the continuity of individual existence as a physical organism, upon this plane of being or any other, was quite beside the point.

> Of such a brother, Ananda, whose heart is thus set free, if any one should say: "His creed is that an Arahant [liberated one] goes on after death," that were absurd. Or: "His creed is that an Arahant does not go on...does, and yet does not, go on...neither goes on nor goes not on after death," all that were absurd.[35]

In the Buddha's original doctrine all metaphysical speculations and all interest in miraculous controls of the physical world are considered not only as beside the point but also as positive hindrances to liberation. It should also be added that the idea of physical reincarnation is no part of Taoism, and that, according to A. K. Coomaraswamy,[36] the proper interpretation of the Vedanta is that "the one and only transmigrant" is the Supreme Self, the Atman-Brahman, and never an individual soul. By such insights the whole reincarnation cosmology of ancient India dissolved either into a myth or into a mere possibility with which one need no longer be concerned. The nightmare of the same individual's repeatedly enduring poverty, disease, and death for aeons of time, or imprisonment for centuries in the torture chambers of demons, came to an end in the realization that there is *no one* to endure it.

What of the claim that liberation confers supernormal powers over the world (*Siddha*)? Where this is not a trick or device (*upaya*) to challenge the student's false assumptions, the interpretation must again be symbolic. The *guru* evades any direct request for miracles by saying that even when one has such powers, they are not to be used to satisfy idle curiosity, and, moreover, that concern with them is a serious obstacle to the attainment of liberation. It should be noted that when anyone has a reputation for extraordinary power or skill of any kind, people will go out of their way to discover it in the ordinary co-incidences of the life that goes on around him, and to interpret perfectly normal events in a supernormal way. The comedian is often one who can so beguile an audience into *expecting* him to be witty that he can set them to bursting their sides with quite ordinary remarks. The philosopher, too, can create a situation in which sheer nonsense or platitudes strike listeners as the greatest profundities, and this may also happen quite without his intention. In the same way, people are positively eager to confirm a particular psychiatrist's reputation for reading their characters like a book, and the whole skill of the fortune-teller is in exploiting the information which his clients let slip in their eagerness to have him read their past and foretell their future. Under such circumstances it is quite useless for the "man of power" to deny his magic, his sanctity, his wit, or his profundity, for a denial will simply be taken as modesty.

The genuine *guru* uses this situation not to make fools of his students but to increase their zeal to dominate the physical world or their own feelings, to act consistently on the false premise that there is a contest between the ego and its experience. For situations of this kind are simply special instances of the double-bind which society puts upon the individual: he *knows* that there are separate events and things, and that he and others are independent agents, just as he *knows* that the comedian's casual remarks are howlingly funny. This is the whole technique of hypnosis, of the judo by which the operator persuades the subject that he cannot disobey him,[37] and in Buddhism liberation is called awakening (*bodhi*) just because it is release from social hypnosis. To be hypnotized is to pretend unconsciously that, say, the hypnotist is invisible, or, comparably, that a game is serious or that "I" am inside my skin and that my field of vision is outside.

But for the symbolic interpretation of supernormal powers let us take, for example, the claim to omnipotence. "I am God, and therefore *everything* that happens is my doing." There is, of course, no way of disproving such an assertion. If I can persuade anyone to believe it, I will have him in a double-bind because he will take me to be willing what would ordinarily be against my will. The only way to escape from the bind is to comment on it, to make a metastatement, as that such an assertion cannot possibly be verified, or that "I do *everything*" is logically equivalent to "I do *nothing*." But the point of ascribing everything that happens to a single agent is to call into question the idea of agency, and at the same time to modify the consciousness of "oneself." In other words, the realization that the ego agent, apart from the act or the choice, is a fiction is equivalent to the feeling that all actions of which you are aware are your own. This feeling is "omnipotence," but it is not actually an awareness of the ego's doing everything. It is awareness of action happening in a unified field, in which it is still possible to observe the conventional difference between "my" deeds and "yours" because they happen at different places in the field. It would mean something to say that I, the ego agent, make choices, perform actions, or think thoughts if it could make any demonstrable difference to what choices and actions occur. But it is *never* demonstrable either that what is done *could* have been done otherwise or that what is done *must* be done — except by confining one's attention to very small fields, by cutting out variables, or, in other words, by taking events out of the context in which they happened. Only by ignoring the full context of an action can it be said either that

I did it freely or that I could not help it. I can try the same action again; if it comes out differently, I say that I could have done it otherwise, but if the same, that I could not. But in the meantime the context has, of course, changed. Because of this the same action can never be repeated.

Now to ignore the context of events is exactly the Buddhist *avidya*, ignorance or ignore-ance, which liberation dispels. In one way the repeatable experiments of science are based on ignore-ance, for they are performed in artificially closed fields. But these experiments add to our knowledge just because the scientist *knows* that he is ignoring. By rigorous isolation of the field he gets more and more detailed knowledge of the way in which fields are, in practice, related to each other. He does not ignore ignore-ance. In the same way the Buddhist discipline overcomes unconscious ignorance — the habitual selective acts of consciousness which screen out "separate" things from their context — by intense concentration. This is judo applied to ignore-ance. The fiction of the ego agent is dispelled by the closest awareness of what actually happens in intending, choosing, deciding, or being spontaneous. One thus comes to understand that consciousness, or attention, *is* ignore-ance and cannot be otherwise. But now one knows it, and thus the *Siddha* of omniscience is not to know everything but to understand the whole process of knowing, to see that all "knowns" are distinguished by ignore-ance. When ignore-ance is unconscious, we take its isolates for realities, and thus the habitual and conventional way of classifying things and events is taken for the natural.

The Buddhist principle that "form is void [*sunya*]" does not therefore mean that there are no forms. It means that forms are inseparable from their context — that the form of a figure is also the form of its background, that the form of a boundary is determined as much by what is outside as by what is inside. The doctrine of *sunyata*, or voidness, asserts only that there are no self-existent forms, for the more one concentrates upon any individual thing, the more it turns out to involve the whole universe. The final Buddhist vision of the world as the *dharmadhatu* — loosely translatable as the "field of related functions" — is not so different from the world view of Western science, except that the vision is experiential rather than theoretical. Poetically, it is symbolized as a vast network of jewels, like drops of dew upon a multidimensional spiderweb. Looking closely at any single jewel, one beholds in it the reflections of all the others. The relationship between the jewels is technically called "thing/thing no obstacle" (*shih shih wu ai*), which is to say that any one form is inseparable from all other forms.

In sum, then, the Buddhist discipline is to realize that anguish or conflict (*duhkha*) arises from the grasping (*trishna*) of entities singled out from the world by ignore-ance (*avidya*) — grasping in the sense of acting or feeling toward them as if they were actually independent of context. This sets in motion the *samsara* or vicious circle of trying to solve the false problem of wresting life from death, pleasure from pain, good from evil, and self from not-self — in short, to get one's ego permanently "one up" on life. But through the meditation discipline the student finds out that he cannot stop this grasping so long as he thinks of himself as the ego which can either act or refrain from action. The attempt *not* to grasp rests upon the same false premise as the grasping: that thinking and doing, intending and choosing, are caused by an ego, that physical events flow from a social fiction. The unreality of the ego is discovered in finding out that there is nothing which it can either do or not do to stop grasping. This insight (*prajna*) brings about *Nirvana*, release from the false problem. But *Nirvana* is a radical transformation of how it feels to be alive: it feels as if everything were myself, or as if everything — including "my" thoughts and actions — were happening of itself. There are still efforts, choices, and decisions, but not in the sense that "I *make* them"; they arise of themselves in relation to circumstances. This is, therefore, to feel life not as an encounter between subject and object, but as a polarized field where the contest of opposites has become the play of opposites.

It is for this reason that Buddhism pairs insight (*prajna*) with compassion (*karuna*), which is the appropriate attitude of the organism to its social and natural environment when it is discovered that the shifting boundary between the individual and the world, which we call the individual's behavior, is common to both. My outline, which is not just the outline of my skin but of every organ and cell in my body, is also the inline of the world. The movements of this outline are my movements, but they are also movements of the world — of its inline. "According to relativity theory, space is not regarded as a container but as a constituent of the material universe."[38] Seeing this, I *feel with* the world. By seeing through the social institution of the separate ego and finding out that my apparent independence was a social convention, I feel all the more one with society. Corresponding, then, to the final vision of the world as a unified field (*dharma-dhatu*), Buddhism sees the fully liberated man as a bodhisattva, as one completely free to take part in the cosmic and social game. When it is said that he is in the world but not of it, that he returns to join in all its activities without attachment, this means that he no longer confuses his identity with his social role — that he plays his role instead of taking it seriously. He is a joker or "wild" man who can play any card in the pack.

His position is thus the same as that of the Atman-Brahman

in Vedanta, of the unclassifiable and unidentifiable Self which plays all the various parts in the cosmic and social drama. As, on a lower level, one is never quite sure who an actor is, since, even when offstage, he may still be acting, so also the bodhisattva has no identity that can be pinned down. "His door stands closed, and the wise ones do not know him. His inner life is hidden, and he moves outside the ruts of the recognized virtues."[39] It is in the same sense that "the foxes have holes and the birds of the air have nests, but the Son of Man has nowhere to lay his head," for the real sense of the homeless life, of being a "forest dweller" (*vanaprastha*) outside caste, is that the role of one's ego is only being played. One's life is an act with no actor, and thus it has always been recognized that the insane man who has lost his mind is a parody of the sage who has transcended his ego. If one is paranoid, the other is metanoid. The sphere of the bodhisattva is thus what Gerald Heard calls "metacomedy," a jargonesque and up-to-date equivalent of the *Divine Comedy*, the viewpoint from which the tragedy of life is seen as comedy because the protagonists are really players. So, too, the lower outcaste, whether criminal or lunatic who cannot be trusted, is always the mirror image of the upper outcaste, the impartial one who takes no sides and cannot be pinned down. But the former retreats from the tragedy of the double-bind because it appears to him to be an insoluble problem. The latter laughs at it because he knows it to be nonsense. When society cannot distinguish between these two outcastes, it treats both alike.

The relation of liberation to social convention becomes clearer still when we pass from India to China. Taoism, the way of liberation, is often described as being fundamentally opposed to Confucianism, the system of social norms, but it is a serious mistake to regard them as mutually exclusive points of view like determinism and free will. Basic to Confucianism is the idea that the proper ordering of society depends upon the "rectification of names," that is, by common agreement as to the definition of roles and their relationships. The Taoist position is that no such definition can be undertaken seriously. Names or words have to be defined with other words, and with what words will these be defined? Therefore the celebrated classic attributed to Lao-tzu, begins:

> *The Tao [Way of nature] that can be told of*
> *Is not the Absolute Tao;*
> *The Names that can be given*
> *Are not Absolute Names.*
> *The Nameless is the origin of Heaven and Earth;*
> *The Named [or, Naming] is the Mother of All Things.*[40]

For things, as we have seen, are units of description, and it is therefore naming and describing which make nature seem to consist of separate units. But

> *Tao was always nameless....*
> *Inasmuch as names are given, one should also*
> *know where to stop.*
> *Knowing where to stop one can become imperishable.*[41]

This "knowing where to stop" is more generally called *wu-wei*, a term whose literal meaning is nonaction or noninterference, but which must more correctly be understood as not acting in conflict with the Tao, the Way or Course of nature. It is therefore against the Tao to try, exhaustively, to pin its unceasing transformations to names, because this will make it appear that the structure of nature is the same as the structure of language: that it is a multitude of distinct things instead of a multitude of changing relations. Because it is the latter, there is actually no way of standing outside nature as to interfere with it. The organism of man does not confront the world but is in the world.

Language *seems* to be a system of fixed terms standing over against the physical events to which they refer. That it is not so, appears in the impossibility of keeping a living language stable. Thinking and knowing seem to be confronting the world as an ego in the same way that words seem to stand over against events; the two illusions stand or fall together. Speaking and thinking are events in and of the physical world, but they are carried on *as if* they were outside it, as if they were an independent and fixed measure with which life could be compared. Hence the notion that the ego can interfere with the world from outside, and can also separate things and events from one another as one can apparently separate "right" (*shih*) from "wrong" (*fei*). Thus Chuang-tzu says:

> How can Tao be so obscured that there should be a distinction of true and false? How can speech be so obscured that there should be a distinction of right [*shih*] and wrong [*fei*]? ... There is nothing which is not *this*; there is nothing which is not *that*. What cannot be seen by *that* [the other person] can be known by myself. Hence I say, *this* emanates from *that*; *that* also derives from *this*. This is the theory of the interdependence of *this* and *that*. Nevertheless, life arises from death, and *vice versa*. Possibility arises from impossibility, and *vice versa*. Affirmation is based upon denial, and *vice versa*. Which being the case, the true sage rejects all distinctions and takes his refuge in Heaven [i.e., in the basic unity of the world].[42]

Taoism, especially in the philosophy of Chuang-tzu, constantly makes fun of Confucian solemnity, of the seriousness with which it is supposed that the right and the wrong can be defined and society put in permanent order. Chuang-tzu related the following (apocryphal) interview between Lao-tzu and Confucius:

> Confucius began to expound the doctrines of his twelve canons, in order to convince Lao-tzu.
>
> "This is all nonsense," cried Lao-tzu, interrupting him. "Tell me what are your criteria."
>
> "Charity," replied Confucius, "and duty towards one's neighbor."...
>
> "Tell me," said Lao-tzu, "in what consist charity and duty to one's neighbor?"
>
> "They consist," answered Confucius, "in a capacity for rejoicing in all things; in universal love, without the element of self. These are the characteristics of charity and duty to one's neighbor."
>
> "What stuff!" cried Lao-tzu. "Does not universal love contradict itself? Is not your elimination of self a positive manifestation of self? Sir, if you would cause the empire not to lose its source of nourishment, — there is the universe, its regularity is unceasing; there are the sun and moon, their brightness is unceasing; there are the stars, their groupings never change; there are birds and beasts, they flock together without varying; there are trees and shrubs, they grow upwards without exception. Be like these; follow Tao; and you will be perfect. Why then these vain struggles after charity and duty to one's neighbor, as though beating a drum in search of a fugitive [who will thus hear you coming and make his escape]. Alas! Sir, you have brought much confusion into the mind of man."[43]

The philosophy of *wu-wei* or noninterference implies, then, the apparently dangerous counsel that people must accept themselves as they are. This will disturb the social order far less than splitting themselves apart to strive after impossible ideals.

> This talk of charity and duty to one's neighbor drives me nearly crazy. Sir, strive to keep the world to its own original simplicity. And as the wind bloweth where it listeth, so let virtue establish itself.... The heron is white without a daily bath. The raven is black without daily coloring itself.[44]

Human nature could be trusted enough to leave itself alone because it was felt to be embedded in the Tao, and the Tao was in turn felt to be a perfectly self-consistent order of nature, manifesting itself in the polarity of *yang* (the positive) and *yin* (the negative). Their polar relationship made it impossible for one to exist without the other, and thus there was no real reason to be for *yang* and against *yin*. If, on the other hand, men do not trust their own nature or the universe of which it is a part, how can they trust their mistrust? Going deeper, what does it mean either to trust or to mistrust, accept or reject oneself, if one cannot actually stand apart from oneself as, say, thinker and thoughts? Will the thinker correct wrong thoughts? But what if the thinker needs to correct the thinker? Is it not simpler to suppose that thoughts may correct themselves?[*]

Chuang-tzu's gentle twitting of Confucian solemnity rises to a genuine humor, almost unique in literature of this kind, because he also makes fun of his own point of view. To do this he employs, in the purest spirit of "meta-comedy," all the analogies between the sage, on the one hand, and the fool, idiot, drunkard,

---

[*] Which indeed they do, by thoughts about thoughts, or language about language, now known as meta-language. Thought is corrected not by a thinker, but rather by further thinking on a higher level.

and wastrel, on the other. As an example of liberation from the dangers of social convention, he idealizes a hideous hunchback who is the first to be rejected by conscription officers and the first to be given a free handout by social service agencies.[45] The sage is as "useless" as a fantastic tree which grew to immense proportions because its fruit was bitter, its leaves inedible, and its trunk and branches so twisted that no one could make planks of it.[46] The way of liberation is "the way down and out"; it is taking, as water does, the course of least resistance; it is by following the natural bent of one's own feelings; it is by becoming stupid and rejecting the refinements of learning; it is by becoming inert and drifting like a leaf on the wind. What is really being said is that intelligence solves problems by seeking the greatest simplicity and the least expenditure of effort, and it is thus that Taoism eventually inspired the Japanese to work out the technique of judo — the easy or gentle Tao (*do*).

There is an obvious parallel here with the philosophy of Carl Rogers's nondirective therapy, in which the therapist simply draws out the logical conclusions of his client's thinking and feeling by doing no more than rephrasing it in what seems to be the clearest form. The responses of the therapist are confined to expressions of his own understanding of what the client says to him. He trusts in the wisdom of the "positive growth potential" of every human being to work out the solution of the problem if only it can be clearly and consistently stated. The therapist himself is therefore "stupid" and "passive" like a Taoist in that he has no theory of what is wrong with his client or what he ought to become in order to be cured. If the client feels that he has a problem, then he has a problem. If he feels that he has no problem, he stops coming for therapy. And the therapist is content in the faith that if the problem is *really* unsolved, the client will eventually return. This is exactly the attitude of a Taoist sage to any would-be student, but its success would seem to depend on whether the therapist is applying a mechanical technique or whether he is genuinely at peace within himself.

The Taoist's position, like Wittgenstein's, is that while there may be logical problems there are no natural, physical problems; nature or Tao is not pursuing any purpose, and therefore is not meeting any difficulties.

> He who replies to one asking about Tao, does not know Tao. Although one may hear about Tao, he does not really hear about Tao. There is no such thing as asking about Tao. There is no such thing as answering such questions. To ask a question which cannot be answered is vain. To answer a question which cannot be answered is unreal. And one who thus meets the vain with the unreal is one who has no physical perception of the universe, and no mental perception of the origin of existence.[47]

This is not because the Tao is inherently mysterious but because the problems of human society are artificial.

> *When the great Tao is lost, spring forth benevolence and*
> *   righteousness.*
> *When wisdom and sagacity arise, there are great hypocrites.*
> *When family relations are no longer harmonious, we have*
> *   filial children and devoted parents.*
> *When a nation is in confusion and disorder, patriots are*
> *   recognized.*[48]

Chuang-tzu therefore compares the liberated man to the "pure men of old," who are supposed to have lived before the artificial aims of society were invented.

> The pure men of old acted without calculation, not seek- ing to secure results. They laid no plans. Therefore, failing,

they had no cause for regret; succeeding, no cause for congratulation. And thus they could scale heights without fear.... They did not know what it was to love life and hate death. They did not rejoice in birth, nor strive to put off dissolution. Quickly come, and quickly go — no more.... This is what is called not to lead the heart astray from Tao, nor to let the human seek to supplement the divine.[49]

Now one might suppose that the Taoists were advocating a romantic primitivism, like the idealization of the noble savage in eighteenth-century Europe. This would be a natural conclusion if the passages quoted are taken entirely out of their social context. But Needham[50] has made a very convincing case for the idea that the artificiality and "technology" to which the Taoists were opposed were those of a feudal system in which the laws were a protection of exploitation, and technology was the manufacture of weapons. Still more important is the fact that Confucianism, despite its undoubted merits, was a scholastic, ritualistic, and purely theoretical conception of the social order without the slightest interest in the order of nature. The whole literature of Taoism shows a deep and intelligent interest in the patterns and processes of the natural world and a desire to model human life upon the observable principles of nature as distinct from the arbitrary principles of a social order resting upon violence.

A violent wind cannot last a whole morning; pelting rain cannot last a whole day. What achieves these things but heaven and earth? Inasmuch as heaven and earth cannot keep up such activity, how much less can man?[51]

In other words, social conventions in direct contradiction with physical patterns cannot support an enduring society. If this is romantic primitivism, psychotherapy is no less so in our own age in advocating ways of life that are consistent with human biology rather than with social tradition. In Confucianism the source of authority was a traditional literature; in Taoism it was the observation of the natural universe, and, as Needham has suggested, there is a close parallel here with the break between Western science, reading the book of nature, and Western scholasticism, reading only the Bible, Aristotle, and St. Thomas Aquinas.

Under any civilized conditions it is, of course, impossible for anyone to act without laying plans, or to refuse absolutely to participate in an economy of waste and violence, whether its ideological sponsorship be capitalist or communist. It is, however, possible to see that this competitive "rat race" need not be taken seriously, or rather, that if we are to persist in it at all it *must* not be taken seriously unless "nervous breakdowns" are to become as common as colds. Bear it in mind that Chuang-tzu's descriptions of the pure men of old and of the life of noninterference are always somewhat exaggerated; they are humorous, like Liang K'ai's paintings of Zen masters.[52]

> The man of character lives at home without exercising his mind and performs actions without worry....Appearing stupid, he goes about like one who has lost his way. He has plenty of money to spend, but does not know where it comes from.[53]

Just as *wu-wei* is not literally doing nothing, liberation is not literally quitting the social game, but treating it as the old man treats the cataract in the following anecdote:

> Confucius was looking at the cataract at Lüliang. It fell from a height of two hundred feet, and its foam reached fifteen miles away. No scaly, finny creature could enter

therein. Yet Confucius saw an old man go in, and thinking that he was suffering from some trouble and desirous of ending his life, bade a disciple run along the side to try and save him. The old man emerged about a hundred paces off, and flowing hair went carolling along the bank. Confucius followed him and said, "I had thought, sir, you were a spirit, but now I see you are a man. Kindly tell me, is there any way to deal thus with water?"

"No," replied the old man, "I have no way.... Plunging in with the whirl, I come out with the swirl. I accommodate myself to the water, not the water to me. And so I am able to deal with it after this fashion."[54]

Between AD 400 and 900 there arose out of the interplay of Taoism and Mahayana Buddhism the school of Ch'an or Zen, with its astonishing technique (of which more will be said later) of teaching liberation by "direct pointing" instead of discussion. The fundamental position of Zen is that it has nothing to say, or, again, that nature is not a problem.

> *The blue hills are simply blue hills;*
> *The white clouds are simply white clouds.*

That is the whole of Zen, and therefore when the student approaches the master with some such artificial question as, "How do I enter the path to liberation?" the master replies, "Do you hear the stream?" "Yes." "There is the way to enter." Or, simpler still, to the question "What is the meaning of Buddhism?" he answers, "Three pounds of flax!" The difficulty of Zen is the almost overwhelming problem of getting anyone to see that life-and-death is *not* a problem. The Zen master tackles this by asking the student to find out *for whom* the world is a problem, for whom is pleasure desirable and pain undesirable, thus turning consciousness back upon itself to discover the ego. But of course it turns out that this mythical "I" that seems to confront experience or to be trapped in the world is nowhere to be found. One day the old Master Sekito found his (very advanced) student Yakusan sitting on a rock. "What are you doing here?" asked Sekito.

"Not one thing," replied Yakusan.

"If so, you are sitting idly."

"Even the sitting idly is doing something."

"You say, 'doing nothing,' but pray what is that which is doing nothing?"

"Even when you call up thousands of wise men, they cannot tell you that."[55]

With their differing methods, Vedanta, Buddhism, and Taoism all involve the realization that life ceases to seem problematic when it is understood that the ego is a social fiction. Sickness and death may be painful, indeed, but what makes them problematic is that they are shameful to the ego. This is the same shame that we feel when caught out of role, as when a bishop is discovered picking his nose or a policeman weeping. For the ego is the role, the "act," that one's inmost self is permanent, that it is in control of the organism, and that while it "has" experiences it is not involved in them. Pain and death expose this pretense, and this is why suffering is almost always attended by a feeling of guilt, a feeling that is all the more difficult to explain when the pretense is unconscious. Hence the obscure but powerful feeling that one *ought* not to suffer or die.

> *You no longer feel quite human.*
> *You're suddenly reduced to the status of an object —*
> *A living object, but no longer a person....*
> *When you've dressed for a party*
> *And are going downstairs, with everything about you*

Arranged to support you in the role you have chosen,
Then sometimes, when you come to the bottom step
There is one step more than your feet expected
And you come down with a jolt. Just for a moment
You have the experience of being an object
At the mercy of a malevolent staircase.[56]

The state of consciousness which follows upon liberation from the ego fiction is quite easily intelligible in neuropsychiatric terms. One of the important physical facts that socialization represses is that all our sensory experiences are states of the nervous system. The field of vision, which we take to be outside the organism, is in fact inside it because it is a translation of the external world into the form of the eye and the optical nerves. What we see is therefore a state of the organism, a state of ourselves. Yet to say even this is to say too much. There is not the external world, and then the state of the nervous system, and then something which sees that state. The seeing is precisely that particular state of the nervous system, a state which for that moment *is* an integral part of the organism. Similarly, one does not hear a sound. The sound is the hearing, apart from which it is simply a vibration in the air. The states of the nervous system need not, as we suppose, be watched by something else, by a little man inside the head who registers them all. Wouldn't he have to have *another* nervous system, and another little man inside *his* head, and so on ad infinitum? When we get an infinite regression of this kind we should always suspect that we have made an unnecessary step in our reasoning. It is the same kind of oscillation that happens when the earpiece of a telephone is placed against the mouthpiece. It "howls."

So, too, when we posit what is in effect a second nervous system watching the first, we are turning the nervous system back upon itself, and thereupon our thoughts oscillate. We become an infinite series of echoes, of selves behind selves behind selves. Now indeed there is a sense in which the cortex is a second nervous system over and above the primary system of the thalamus. Oversimplifying things considerably, we could say that the cortex works as an elaborate feedback system for the thalamus by means of which the organism can to some extent be aware of itself. Because of the cortex, the nervous system can know that it knows; it can *re*cord and *re*cognize its own states. But this is just one "echo," not an infinite series. Furthermore, the cortex is just another neural pattern, and its states are neural patterns; it is not something other than neural pattern as the ego agent is supposed to be, in the organism but not of it.

How can the cortex observe and control the cortex? Perhaps there will come a day when the human brain will fold back on itself again and develop a higher cortex, but until then the only feedback which the cortex has about its own states comes through other people. (I am speaking here of the cortex as a whole. One can, of course, remember remembering.) Thus the ego which observes and controls the cortex is a complex of social information relayed back into the cortex — Mead's "generalized other." But this is social misinformation when it is made to appear that the information of which the ego consists is something other than states of the cortex itself, and therefore ought to be controlling the cortex. The ego is the unconscious pretense that the organism contains a higher system than the cortex; it is the confusion of a system of interpersonal information with a new, and imaginary, fold in the brain — or with something quite other than a neural pattern, a mind, soul, or self. When, therefore, I feel that "I" am knowing or controlling myself — my cortex — I should recognize that I am actually being controlled by other people's words and gestures masquerading as my inner or better self. Not to see this brings about utter confusion, as when I try to force myself to stop feeling in ways that are socially objectionable.

If all this is true, it becomes obvious that the ego feeling is pure hypnosis. Society is persuading the individual to do what it wants by making it appear that its commands are the individual's inmost self. What we want is what you want. And this is a double-bind, as when a mother says to her child, who is longing to slush around in a mud puddle, "Now, darling, you don't *want* to get into that mud!" This is misinformation, and this — if anything — is the "Great Social Lie."

Let us suppose, then, that the false reflex of "I seeing my sights" or "I feeling my feelings" is stopped by such methods as the ways of liberation employ. Will it not thereupon become clear that all our perceptions of the external world are states of the organism? The division between "I" and "my sights" is projected outwardly into the sharp division between the organism and what it sees. Just such a change of perception as this would explain the feeling, so usual at the moment of liberation (*satori*), that the external world is oneself and that external actions are one's own doing. Perception will then be known for what it is, a field relationship as distinct from an encounter.* It is hardly too much to say that such a change of perception would give

---

* I am reasonably satisfied that something approximating this change of perception, the realization that sensations are states of the organism itself, is brought about by lysergic acid (LSD-25). Many drugs suspend inhibitions that are useful, but it seems that LSD suspends an inhibition which is of very doubtful value, and thus its use as a therapeutic might be explored further on the hypothesis that this is the main feature of its action. Elsewhere[17] I have discussed more fully the partial resemblances between the LSD experience and "cosmic consciousness."

far better ground for social solidarity than the normal trick of misinformation and hypnosis.

There is one further question which should be raised at this point, a question that repeatedly comes up in any discussion of the usefulness of the ways of liberation to the psychotherapist. Despite Freud's own basic prudishness, the whole history of psychotherapy is bound up with a movement toward sexual freedom in Western culture. This seems to be in sharp conflict with the fact that the ways of liberation so largely enjoin celibacy and the monastic or eremitic life upon their followers. Many texts could be cited to show that sexual passion is held to be a major obstacle to liberation.

To understand this, we must first go back to the social context of liberation in ancient India. In the normal course of things, no one entered upon these disciplines until the latter part of his life. In the various *ashramas* or stages of life the liberative stage of "forest dweller" (*vanaprastha*) came only after completion of the stage of "householder" (*grihastha*). No one was expected to seek liberation until he had raised a family and handed over his occupation to his sons. It was assumed that liberation was not only freedom from social convention but also from social responsibility. Mahayana Buddhism was to modify this idea radically, and we shall see that the answer to our problem lies here rather than in the disciplines that remain inseparable from Hindu culture — Vedanta and Yoga. But it is significant that Jung, too, regards the individuation process of his psychotherapy as a task for the second half of life, as a preparation for death.

In all ancient precontraceptive societies sexual activity is obviously inseparable from procreation, and thus from several points of view it seemed unsuitable for a man in the stage of *vanaprastha* to become a father. In an age when life expectancy was far shorter than it is today, there was slight chance that he would live to raise his children to maturity. Furthermore, there was a potential conflict between the duty of socializing the children and liberating himself. It must also be remembered that primitive physiology associates the seminal emission with a "loss" of vital fluid comparable to a loss of blood, confusing the relaxation of detumescence with impaired vitality. Hence the widespread but quite fallacious notion that "Every animal is sad after intercourse [*Omne animal triste post coitum*]." But, apart from all these considerations, the main reason for insisting upon the repression of sexual desire was that this offered a major challenge to the reality of the ego, as if to say, "If you can thwart your biological nature, you really do exist!"

This is such a drastic method of challenging the ego that, as with certain potent drugs, one is justified in using it only if fairly certain that it will work. Indeed, all the methods of liberation were supposed to work and therefore to be *temporary* disciplines. The Buddhist discipline is often likened to a raft for crossing from the shore of *samsara* to the shore of *Nirvana*, and the texts say again and again that when the farther shore is reached the raft should be left behind. In Mahayana Buddhism, as we have seen, the liberated bodhisattva returns from the forest or hermitage into society and the world. But the practical difficulty is that in Asia the ways of liberation are, with some exceptions, as inefficient and as theoretically confused as psychotherapy in the West. Indeed, the whole point of comparing them with psychotherapy is to effect a mutual clarification. Chronic Buddhism is perhaps even more common than chronic psychotherapy — twice a week for twenty years or more.

For, as things actually work out, followers of the ways in modern Asia seem to have lost their nerve to such an extent that one rarely hears of anyone actually being liberated outside the particular discipline of Zen Buddhism. (Perhaps other schools are more modest, and, indeed, there is a certain contradiction in saying "*I* am liberated" if the ego is unreal. But there is also the false modesty of so imitating humility that it becomes more important to be humble than to be liberated. Golden chains are as binding as chains of iron. There are also followers of the ways who remain anonymous and unorganized — Taoists, for example, who simply mind their own business and lay no claim to anything at all save, with a certain humor, stupidity.) But the general loss of nerve is due in part to what might be called the distance of excessive reverence. Whenever a tradition becomes venerable with the passage of time, the ancient masters and sages are elevated to pedestals of sanctity and wisdom which lift them far above the human level. The way of liberation becomes confused with a popular cult; the ancient teachers become gods and supermen, and thus the ideal of liberation or Buddhahood becomes ever more remote. No one believes that it can be reached except by the most unusually gifted and heroic prodigies. Consequently the medicine of the discipline becomes a diet, the cure an addiction, and the raft a houseboat. In this manner, a way of liberation turns into just another social institution and dies of respectability.

Outside the sphere of influence of Mahayana Buddhism this has happened so widely that being on the way to liberation is the most that anyone expects. The few liberated ones to be recognized are freaks of birth, like Sri Ramakrishna or Sri Ramana Maharshi, or very old men like the late Sri Aurobindo. But under these circumstances what was intended as a swift remedy, the effort to repress sexuality, becomes chronic prudery, and it is thus forgotten or simply hushed up that the bodhisattva is not expected to be celibate. Nor, on the other hand, is he likely to be a libertine since he does not need to use sexual release as an escape from the "problem" of life. It is important, too, to remember that, outside the supposedly temporary discipline of liberation, the sexual mores of Asian cultures are in many ways far more liberal than ours, and the association of sexuality with sin is rare indeed. Thus the sexual expression of the bodhisattva is limited only by his own sense of good taste and by the customs of whatever secular society may be his home. The "graduate" of a Zen community may therefore become a married priest or simply return into lay life.*

There is good reason to believe that liberated sexuality might be something like a mature form of what Freud so inappropriately called the "polymorphous perverse" sexuality of the infant, that is, an erotic relationship of organism and environment that is not restricted to the genital system.[65] The eyes and

---

* This is not the place to enter into the very special problem of the Tantric use of sexuality in the actual discipline of liberation. The reader is referred to Dasgupta,[58] Eliade,[59] and Woodroffe[60] for highly reliable accounts, and to my own more conjectural interpretation.[61] But as to the permissibility of sexuality for the bodhisattva or liberated man, many texts are perfectly explicit. E.g., *Chandogya Upanishad*, 8. 12. 3., "Man issues forth from bodily identification to assume his real form upon attainment of the great illumination. Such a man is best among men. He lives like a king — eating, playing, and enjoying women, possessions, and family, without identification with the body." *Subhashita-samgraha*, 47, "Foolish people think of liberation as something entirely different from the enjoyment of the world; but whatever there is sublime and great which is heard, seen, smelt, eaten, known, and touched, is good all round.... The whole drama of the world is to be known as perfectly pure by nature."[62] *Saraha-pada*, 19, "Without meditating, without renouncing the world, / One may stay at home in the company of one's wife. / Can that be called perfect knowledge, Saraha says, / If one is not released while enjoying the pleasures of sense?"[63] Modern Indian spirituality, especially among the classes affected by Western-style education, is heavily tinged with (presumably) British puritanism, but the best discussion of this whole problem is that by A. K. Coomaraswamy.[64]

the ears, the nose and the skin, all become avenues of erotic communion, not just with other people, but with the whole realm of
nature, for genital eroticism is simply a special canalization of
the basic love which is the polarity of *yang* and *yin*. The texts say
repeatedly that the bodhisattva is free to enter into the relationship of love because he is unattached. This does *not* mean that
he enters into it mechanically, with feelings as cold as ice. Nor
is this the sort of subterfuge whereby some religious libertines
have justified anything that they do by explaining that all physical states are illusory, or that their "spirit" is really above it all.
The point is rather that such sexuality is completely genuine and
spontaneous (*sahaja*); its pleasure is detached in the sense that
it is not compulsively sought out to assuage anxiety, to prove
one's manliness, or to serve as a substitute for liberation. "Sahaja," wrote Coomaraswamy, "has nothing to do with the cult
of pleasure. It is a doctrine of the Tao, and a path of non-pursuit.
All that is best for us comes of itself into our hands — but if we
strive to overtake it, it perpetually eludes us."[66]

IV. THROUGH A GLASS DARKLY

It is perfectly natural that man himself should be the most un-intelligible part of the universe. The way his organism looks to an outside observer, such as a neurosurgeon, is so astonishingly different from the way it feels from the inside. The way in which human behavior is described by the biologist or the sociologist is so unlike what is seen by the ordinary individual that he can hardly recognize himself. But the disparity is no different in principle from the shock of hearing for the first time a recording of one's own voice or from getting a frank description of one's character from a shrewd observer. These descriptions, like the whole external world itself, seem so foreign, so *other*. Yet the time may come when the shock of strangeness turns into the shock of recognition, when looking at the external world as a mirror we may exclaim with amazement, "Why, that's *me!*"

Collectively, we are still a long way from this recognition. The world beyond us is an alien and unfathomable unknown, and we look into its glass very darkly indeed, confronting it as though we did not belong.

I, a stranger, and afraid,
In a world I never made.

Only slowly does it dawn upon us that there is something fundamentally wrong with this feeling; simple logic, if nothing else, forces us to see that however separated self and other may be, there is no self without this other. But standing in the way of this recognition is the fear of finding out that this external world may be *only* oneself, and that the answer to one's voice is only an endless reverberation of echoes. This is, of course, because our conception of self is confined to a very small and mainly fictitious part of our being, and to discover that the world were a belt of mirrors round *that* taper's flame would indeed be a horrifying solipsism. Yet if it turns out that self and other are one, it will also turn out that self and surprise are one.

We have been seeing all along that although Western science started out by trying to gain the greatest objectivity, the greatest lack of involvement between the observer and the observed, the more diligently this isolation is pressed, the more impossible it is found to be. From physics to psychology, every department of science is realizing more and more that to observe the world is to participate in it, and that, frustrating as this may first seem to be, it is the most important clue of all to further knowledge. At the same time, it is often pointed out that there is an ever-widening gap of communication between the scientific specialist and the lay public because his language is incomprehensible and his models of the world ever more remote from the images of common sense. Another aspect of this gap is that the world as we are coming to know it theoretically bears little resemblance to the world that we feel: we have sixteenth-century personalities in the world of twentieth-century concepts because social conventions lag far behind the flight of theoretical knowledge.

Is it possible, however, that science will become Western man's way of liberation? Such an idea is about as repugnant as anything can be to most exponents of the traditional Eastern ways, who are apt to regard science as the very nadir of Western materialism. Thus one of the most gifted interpreters of the Vedanta, René Guénon, writes:

> The domain of every science is always dependent upon experimentation, in one or other of its various modalities, whereas the domain of metaphysic [i.e., liberation] is essentially constituted by that of which no external investigation is possible: being "beyond physics" we are also, by that very fact, beyond experiment. Consequently, the field of every separate science can, if it is capable of it, be extended indefinitely without ever finding the slightest point of contact with the metaphysical sphere.[67]

But the world of knowledge may, like the earth, be round — so that an immersion in material particulars may quite unexpectedly lead back to the universal and the transcendent. Blake's idea that "the fool who persists in his folly will become wise" is the same as Spinoza's "the more we know of particular things, the more we know of God." For this, as we have seen, was the essential technique of liberation: to encourage the student to explore his false premises consistently — to the end. Unhappily, most Western devotees of the Eastern ways know little or nothing of what has happened in science during the last fifty years, and they think of it still as the reduction of the world to the "objects" of Newtonian mechanics.*

It is true that the historical origins of applied science lay in Western man's exaggerated feeling of estrangement from nature, and that in many ways his technology is still an attack upon the world. Psychoanalysts galore have pointed out the degree to which the objective, rigorous, analytical, and parsimonious spirit of science is an expression of hostility, an attempt to render the physical world perfectly sterile. No one but us objects around here! Everything is scrubbed clean of mystery until it is quite dead, and the universe is explained away as "nothing but" mechanism and fortuitous arrangements of blind energy. But one cannot persist in such hostility without discovering that something is wrong, just as a social group cannot annihilate its enemy without discovering that it has lost a friend. As Norman Brown puts it:

> Whitehead and Needham are protesting against the inhuman attitude of modern science; in psychoanalytical terms, they are calling for a science based on an erotic sense of reality, rather than an aggressive dominating attitude toward reality.... The mentality which was able to reduce nature to "a dull affair, soundless, scentless, colourless; merely the hurrying of material endlessly, meaninglessly" — Whitehead's description — is lethal. It is an awe-inspiring attack on the life of the universe; in more technical psychoanalytical terms, its anal-sadistic intent is plain.[68]

But he goes on to quote the psychoanalytically oriented historian of science, Gaston Bachelard, in a passage which curiously

---

* It would not be fair to say so without admitting that I myself have labored under the same ignorance, as any informed reader of *The Supreme Identity* will see.

misinterprets the twentieth-century revolution in scientific description:

> It does indeed seem that with the twentieth century there begins a kind of scientific thought in opposition to the senses, and that it is necessary to construct a theory of objectivity *in opposition to* the object.... It follows that the entire use of the brain is being called into question. From now on the brain is strictly no longer adequate as an instrument for scientific thought; that is to say, the brain is the *obstacle* to scientific thought. It is an obstacle in the sense that it is the coordinating center for human movements and appetites. It is necessary to think *in opposition to* the brain.[69]

At a time when the electronic computer is taking over so much of the burden of thought and when, as we have said, physical models of the universe appear to be sensuously inconceivable, Bachelard's words are persuasive. This is the more so when the practical outcome of modern physics may be the actual destruction of life upon this planet. But Bachelard does not see that what science is now overcoming is a type of sense perception and a whole image of the world that was itself in opposition to the senses and the organism. Newton's mechanical universe was far more inhuman than Einstein's relative universe. Descartes's firm dichotomy of subject and object, ego and world, was far more antiorganic than modern field theory. And what about the still earlier conceptions of the body and the physical world as the domain of corruption and evil? Indeed, when we look through the microscope, as when we look at the art of Picasso, Klee, or Pollock, the human body is not there in its familiar form. Kepes's *New Landscape*[70] and similar works present both the macroscopic and microscopic forms of nature revealed by scientific instruments as objects for aesthetic contemplation, and who can deny their incomparable beauty?

But this is not necessarily, in Berdyaev's phrase, "the destruction of the human image." It is certainly not the image of man as it was seen by painters of the Renaissance and, still less, of *l'art officiel* of the nineteenth century. For this was an image which stressed above all the separation of man from his surroundings, an art in which man was defined and bounded by his skin, and in which conventional perspective stressed the distance of the subject from the object. But when we compare Kepes's photographs with the Islamic arabesque, with Chinese calligraphy, or with the fantastic border ornaments of Celtic manuscripts, is the resemblance quite fortuitous? Indeed, this new landscape is unfamiliar, but with one more turn of the screw on the microscope we shall again see ourselves. We shall look a little longer at the photographs from Palomar, and the shape of the cosmos will be seen, perhaps quite suddenly, to be the shape of man: it will make *sense*. It will not, however, be the shape of the ego, of the purely abstract and conceptual man who is locked up inside his skin.

We might say that the more unfamiliar, the more *other* the form in which man learns to recognize himself, the deeper his knowledge of himself becomes — reversing the Delphic aphorism into "Know the universe and the gods, and thou shalt know thyself." If, then, man is to rediscover his own image in the macroscopic and microscopic worlds which science reveals, this will be the "own image" in which God is said to have created him — that is, the universal man, the Adam-Kadmon, the Son of Man, or the universe considered as the Body of Buddha (*buddhakaya*). These are mythological symbols, and however poetic and anthropomorphic they may seem to be, their meaning is the fact upon which exact science has now stumbled: that the part and the whole, the individual and the cosmos, are what they are only in relation to one another. The hitherto unconscious or socially ignored form of man is the form of the world. As Whitehead puts it:

> Appearances are finally controlled by the functionings of the animal body. These functionings and the happenings within the contemporary regions [i.e., environments of the body] are both derived from a common past, highly relevant to both. It is thereby pertinent to ask, whether the animal body and the external regions are not attuned together, so that under normal circumstances, the appearances conform to natures within the regions. The attainment of such conformation would belong to the perfection of nature in respect to the higher types of animal life.... We have to ask whether nature does not contain within itself a tendency to be in tune, an Eros urging towards perfection.[71]

Is not this at least the beginning of an answer to the hope which Freud expresses at the end of *Civilization and Its Discontents?*

> Men have brought their powers of subduing the forces of nature to such a pitch that by using them they could now very easily exterminate one another to the last man. They know this — hence arises a great part of their current unrest, their dejection, their mood of apprehension. And now it may be expected that the other of the two "heavenly forces," eternal Eros, will put forth his strength so as to maintain himself alongside of his equally immortal adversary.[72]

"And," adds Norman Brown, "perhaps our children will live to live a full life, and to see what Freud could not see — in the old adversary [Thanatos], a friend."[73]

But if science is actually to become our way of liberation, its theoretical view must be translated into feeling, not only for laymen but also for scientists themselves. Shortly after I had read one of the most fascinating accounts of this new unitary view of man-in-the-world, *The Next Development in Man*,[74] by the British biophysicist L. L. Whyte, I put this very problem to the author. He replied that it had never occurred to him and that, so far as he was concerned, the feeling should naturally follow from a thorough comprehension of the theory. I was asking, in other words, whether science should not comprise a yoga — a discipline for realizing its view as what psychologists call *insight*, over and above verbal understanding. There may be some truth in what Whyte said. After all, when it has been pointed out to us that the following two-dimensional figure is a cube, we really feel it to be so.

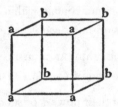

But it is extremely difficult to point out insights which go against common sense and social standards of sanity, just as it is difficult for the convention of perspective to suggest depth to a member of a culture in which it is not used. By what effort can *we* see at a single glance that the above figure is two cubes, one of which has the square with corners *a* in front, and the other the square with corners *b*? Can we see two different facts as one?[75] To be truly liberative, Western science must have its own yoga, and some outgrowth of psychotherapy is the natural candidate for the task. The question is whether the kind of psychotherapy that we know is in any position to fulfill it, even for the small minority that can be reached by its consultative method.

There are, indeed, a number of ways in which science and psychotherapy have already been liberative, in the strict sense of enabling people to see the contradictory or fictitious character of some social institutions. With a somewhat different approach, science has done to the Christian cosmology of Dante and St. Thomas what Buddhism did to the reincarnation cosmology of ancient India: it has exorcised its terrors and also made it thoroughly implausible. It is not by any means that science has disproved the existence of God the Father, Heaven and Hell, the hosts of angels, and the resurrection of the body. On the one hand, modern astronomical, physical, and biological knowledge makes this cosmology simply inappropriate. In comparison with the new image of the universe, the traditional Christian image is naive, and theologians can save it only by tortuous feats of sophistication. On the other hand, historical research makes evident that its origins were something very different from divine revelation. The concept of God the Father was, as Whitehead says, "a sublimation from its barbaric origin. He stood in the same relation to the whole World as early Egyptian or Mesopotamian kings stood to their subject populations. Also the moral characters were very analogous."[76]

Science and psychotherapy have also done much already to liberate us from the prison of isolation from nature in which we were supposed to renounce Eros, despise the physical organism, and rest all our hopes in a supernatural world — to come later. But that this liberation is by no means complete is clear from the fact that nineteenth-century naturalism was the basis for a technological assault on nature without precedent in history. This liberation is, in other words, a very partial affair even for the small minority which has fully understood and accepted it. It leaves us still as strangers in the cosmos — without the judgment of God but without his love, without the terrors of Hell but without the hope of Heaven, without many of the physical agonies of prescientific times but without the sense that human life has any meaning. The Christian cosmos has vanished, but the Christian ego remains — with no resort but to try to forget its loneliness in some sort of collectivism, of huddling together in the dark.

Can psychotherapy complete the job? In almost all its forms it has one enormous asset: the realization that escape is no answer, that the shudders, horrors, and depressions in which "the problem of life" is manifested must be explored and their roots felt out. We must get rid of the idea that we ought not to have such feelings, and the relatively new Existential school goes so far as to say that anxiety and guilt are inseparable from human life; to be, consciously, is to know that being is relative to non-being, and that the possibility of ceasing to be is present at every moment and certain in the end. Here is the root of *angst*, the basic anguish of being alive which is approximately the Buddhist *duhkha*, the chronic suffering from which the Buddha proposed deliverance. To be or not to be is *not* the question; to be *is* not to be. Because of anxiety man is never fully possessed of what Tillich calls "the courage to be," and for this he always feels guilt; he has never been completely true to himself.* This is one example of the fact that the strength of our psychotherapies lies

---

* I am not sure whether the Existentialists' complete acceptance of *angst* is intended, by indirection, to annul it — overcoming it by *allowing* it to be. Rollo May[77] states that the aim of existential therapy is to enable the patient to experience his own existence, his being-in-the-world, fully and authentically. When one's existence is not confronted with the constant possibility of nonexistence, it is taken for granted — i.e., it is not taken seriously. Is not this the old Christian principle of "Live every day as if thy last"? But this is still something different from the serenity of the one who is "already dead," who is completely willing not to be. Unfortunately May does not discuss this — and he is one of the very few representatives of the school whose writing begins to be readable!

in their attitudes rather than in their theories and techniques. Or, as George Mora has put it:

> We find increasing acknowledgement of the fact that psy-chotherapeutic results are strikingly similar regardless of the theoretical framework followed by each therapist, that the personality of the therapist is more important than his adherence to a particular school of thought.[78]

The logical counterpart of the attitude that escape is no answer is the attitude of the acceptance of all "psychological reality" by the therapist and, in turn, by the patient, whether it be aesthetically or morally objectionable or contrary to sane ideas of what reality is. Perhaps this has been most eloquently expressed by Jung, speaking before a group of ministers back in 1932:

> We cannot change anything unless we accept it. Con-demnation does not liberate, it oppresses....If a doctor wishes to help a human being he must be able to accept him as he is. And he can do this in reality only when he has already seen and accepted himself as he is. Perhaps this sounds very simple, but simple things are always the most difficult. In actual life it requires the greatest art to be simple, and so acceptance of oneself is the essence of the moral problem and the acid test of one's whole outlook on life. That I feed the beggar, that I forgive an insult, that I love my enemy in the name of Christ — all these are undoubtedly great virtues. What I do unto the least of my brethren, that I do unto Christ. But what if I should discover that the least amongst them all, the poorest of all beggars, the most impudent of all offenders, yea the very fiend himself — that these are within me, and that I myself stand in need of the alms of my own kindness,

> that I myself am the enemy who must be loved — what
> then? ... Had it been God himself who drew near to us in
> this despicable form, we should have denied him a thou-
> sand times before a single cock had crowed.[79]

To have "seen and accepted himself as he is" appears, then, to be
that essential quality of personality which, as Mora says, is more
important for the therapist than his theory or school. Though it
sounds simple, and not very heroic, its implications are tremendous and its difficulties extraordinary — for what constitutes
"myself" and who is it that accepts me? This is no mere matter
of bringing about a reconciliation between the ego and a number
of repressed experiences, shameful or painful but always contents of one's own subjectivity. It is the much larger problem of
integrating the split which has come about between the individual and the world, and, as we have seen, this has little to do with
adjusting him to society.

Speaking quite generally, this is the point at which psychotherapy falls short of being a way of liberation, even when
it is recognized that therapy is far more than adjustment. The
weakness lies not so much in the theoretical differences and confusions of the various schools as in certain tacit agreements —
in particular the continued acceptance of the dualistic view of
man: ego and unconscious, psyche and soma, subject and object, reality principle and pleasure principle, reason and instinct.
Therapy is healing, making whole, and any system which leaves
the individual upon one horn of the dualistic dilemma is at best
the achievement of courageous despair. This is just what Freud
himself came to; his later writings reflect the deep pessimism of a
very brave man, for he felt that the conflict between the pleasure
principle, Eros, and the demands of the reality principle, of the

necessities of civilization, was irreconcilable. For its own survival Eros must be regulated, civilized, and repressed, but

> ...the repressed instinct never ceases to strive for complete satisfaction, which would consist in the repetition of a primary experience of satisfaction. No substitutive or reactive formations and no sublimations will suffice to remove the repressed instinct's persisting tension.[80]

As the social obligations of the individual grow larger and civilized life requires more and more discipline, the situation gets worse.

> If civilization is an inevitable course of development from the group of the family to the group of humanity as a whole, then an intensification of the sense of guilt...will be inextricably bound up with it, until perhaps the sense of guilt may swell to a magnitude that individuals can hardly support.[81]

But the problem is insoluble because of the way in which it is posed. The great irreconcilables, pleasure principle and reality principle, Eros and Thanatos, rest upon the deeper duality of the knower and the known which Freud took for granted because it was the primary assumption of his culture — even though he saw so clearly that the ego is not master in its own house. He saw that the ego arises out of the tension between the libido and culture; he knew, in other words, that the ego is a social artifact. But he regarded it as essential to consciousness; there could be no knowing, no control of human affairs, no science or art, without the opposition of the knower to the known — that is, of civilized order to nature and of the ego to the unconscious. Thus all that is distinctively human is against nature even though — and here is the conflict — inseparable from it. Eros *cannot* be put down

but it *must* be. Nature is boundless lust and rapacity, and man
has evolved from it through the ruthless struggle of natural selection. Although it was now clear from biology that consciousness had grown out of the unconscious, the ego from the id, this
must be regarded as a natural accident. Left to itself, the unconscious evolution of the ego could not be expected to go any
further, because nature was inherently unintelligent. Nature's
accident, man, must be seized from inevitable dissolution by
proceeding to act as if reason were opposed to nature. In practice, then, to regard man as a natural accident, whose survival is
thenceforth inconsistent with nature, amounts to the same thing
as regarding him as an intelligence outside nature. This is why
nineteenth-century naturalism, the assumptions of which Freud
shared, simply intensified the traditional split between spirit and
nature.

Yet, as L. L. Whyte has shown in his critique of Freud, all
this is bad biology.

> In biological development dualism or conflict is always
> superimposed on a prior unity. The existence of an organ-
> ism capable of survival implies integration and unity is
> therefore always prior to inner conflict. Conflict may arise
> as the result of an inappropriate adaptation, and it may
> prove fatal or it may be overcome. But the recovery of
> organic health never involves the synthesis of fundamen-
> tally opposed principles, since these cannot co-exist in an
> organism. It only seems to do so because the actual con-
> dition of the organism has been misinterpreted in using a
> dualistic language. The historical process does not involve
> the synthesis of pre-existing logical opposites, though it
> may appear to in the confused language of immature dia-
> lectical theories.[82]

In other words, Freud did not see that the ego was an inappropriate adaptation. He saw that, as a social convention, it was self-contradictory, but he did not see that it was unnecessary. He could not conceive of consciousness without the duality of subject and object.*

With all his knowledge of Eastern thought, Jung seems to be in no better position.

> The Eastern mind, however, has no difficulty in conceiving of a consciousness without an ego. Consciousness is deemed capable of transcending its ego condition; indeed, in its "higher" forms, the ego disappears altogether. Such an ego-less mental condition can only be unconscious to us, for the simple reason that there would be nobody to witness it....I cannot imagine a conscious mental state that does not refer to a subject, that is, to an ego. The ego may be depotentiated — divested, for instance, of its awareness of the body — but so long as there is awareness of something, there must be somebody who is aware.[84]

How a mere convention of syntax, that the verb must have a subject, can force itself upon perception and seem to be the logic of reality! Under these circumstances Jung's understanding of the

---

* Yet how often he came so close to the point! One thinks, in particular, of his remarkable little essay "The Antithetical Sense of Primal Words,"[83] where he reviews Karl Abel's studies of the polarity of such words as the ancient Egyptian *ken*, meaning both strong and weak. Freud had noticed a similar ambivalence or polarity in the symbolism of dreams. "Dreams," he wrote in the same essay, "show a special tendency to reduce two opposites to a unity or to represent them as one thing." He goes on to quote Abel, "It is clear that everything on this planet is relative and has independent existence only in so far as it is distinguished in its relations to and from other things....Man has not been able to acquire even his oldest and simplest conceptions otherwise than in contrast with their opposite; he only gradually learnt to separate the two sides of the antithesis and think of the one without conscious comparison with the other."

"ego-less" state of consciousness as the Eastern texts describe it leaves much to be desired. To put it rather briefly, he believes that it is not ego-less at all.[85] It is only that the ego is temporarily forgotten in descending to a more primitive level of awareness, to the undifferentiated awareness that is supposed to have been characteristic of man's precivilized mentality — Lévy-Bruhl's *participation mystique*. However, he does not confuse it with an actual reversion to primitivity. His point is that members of the ancient Eastern cultures can afford this relapse into undifferentiated awareness just because of their maturity, just because their cultures have given them very strong ego structures and have at the same time provided for the ordered fulfillment of all their instinctual urges.[86] This is why he strongly discourages the use of Eastern techniques, such as yoga, by Westerners. For us there is the danger of "inflation," of being swamped and possessed by the unconscious just because we have repressed it so strongly and have not yet come to terms with our less respectable instincts. The Westerner who lowers the level of consciousness and relaxes the vigilance of the ego, without all the safeguards of the analytic situation, is therefore liable to lose self-control in the uprush of repressed forces. One thinks immediately of the "beat" variety of Zen in America's bohemias, and the delusions of spiritual and occult grandeur among some of those who take up Theosophy or Vedanta.

There are so many points upon which Jung has such excellent intuitive judgment that one hates to take issue with his premises. In East and West alike there is always a danger of disorder when social institutions are called in question, and it is the same whether the institution be the ego or the subjugation of women. When authority is questioned at one point, it tends to become unstable at others. East and West alike have fostered the ego as such an institution, though with differing ideas of its roles and duties. If Eastern cultures were less ego-conscious than Western, then Buddhist and Taoist texts would be relatively silent as to the illusory nature of the ego. Jung is therefore perfectly right in sounding a warning — but for the wrong reason. He assumes that a strong ego structure, a struggle against nature, is the necessary condition of civilization, and is thus in danger of reaching the same despair as Freud. But it is one thing to note that civilization as we know it *has* depended upon the ego concept; it is quite another to assert that it *must*, as if this convention were somehow in the nature of things. Freud and Jung are both fully alive to the interdependence of life's great opposites, but for both they constitute a finally insoluble problem. Freud fears that the tension between them must at least become unbearable; Jung seems prepared to walk the tightrope between them forever.

> The serious problems of life, however, are never fully solved. If it should for once appear that they are, this is the sign that something has been lost. The meaning and design of a problem seem not to lie in its solution but in our working at it incessantly. This alone preserves us from stultification and petrifaction.[87]

Is not this, after all, the voice of the Protestant conscience? Man is inherently lazy; by nature, by original sin, he will always slide back into dissolution unless there is something to goad him, and thus there must never, never be anything but quite temporary rest from the task of working out his salvation with fear and trembling.

Maslow[88] has amassed a most impressive series of quotations from American psychologists, one and all averring the identity of problem solving, or "coping," and mental health, and to read them thus lumped into a chorus is downright funny.

> Western culture generally [writes Maslow] rests on the
> Judaic-Christian theology. The United States particularly
> is dominated by the Puritan and pragmatic spirit which
> stresses work, struggle and striving, soberness and ear-
> nestness, and above all, purposefulness. Like any other
> social institution, science in general and psychology in
> particular is not exempt from these cultural climate and at-
> mosphere effects. American psychology, by participation,
> is overpragmatic, over-Puritan, and overpurposeful....
> No textbooks have chapters on fun and gaiety, on leisure
> and meditation, on loafing and puttering, on aimless, use-
> less, and purposeless activity....American psychology is
> busily occupying itself with only half of life to the neglect
> of the other — and perhaps more important — half.[89]

In all directions we use the means of life to justify the ends: we
read or go to concerts to improve our minds; we relax to improve our work; we worship God to improve our morals; we
even get drunk *in order to* forget our worries. Everything that
is done playfully, without ulterior motive and second thought,
makes us feel guilty, and it is even widely believed that such unmotivated action is impossible. You *must* have a reason for what
you do! But the statement is more of a command than an observation. As soon as the ego is divided from the world, like the
effect from its cause, it seems to be the puppet of "motivations"
which are really the disowned parts of ourselves. If we could see
ourselves whole, as differing positions in the unified field of the
world, we should see that we are unmotivated — for the whole
floats freely and does not rest upon something beyond itself.

Jung and his students have shown such a deep interest in
Asian philosophy and mythology that their defective understanding of liberation cannot be passed over lightly. They come

so close to the point, and yet miss it, and there may be something here which is symptomatic of the whole situation of Western psychotherapy vis-à-vis the Eastern ways. The difficulty seems to arise from three interconnected factors: (1) the Christian and more particularly Protestant view of man; (2) anthropological theories of the nineteenth century; and (3) "psychologism."

As we have seen, our Western and Christian social institutions define man in a way that is not only paradoxical but also self-contradictory. Man is seen as an embodied conflict between reason and instinct, spirit and nature, such that to be healthy or to be saved he must always mistrust himself. Jung does not show this contradiction as acutely as Freud because he holds that the unconscious is at root creative and intelligent, and thus *ultimately* trustworthy.* The mythologies, dreams, and fantasies which represent unconscious activity are regarded as sources of healing and wisdom, and are comparable to the processes of growth and homeostasis in the physical organism. Nevertheless, Jungian writings abound in such passages as the following from M. E. Harding:

> Beneath the decent facade of consciousness with its disciplined, moral order and its good intentions, lurk the crude instinctive forces of life, like monsters of the deep — devouring, begetting, warring endlessly. They are for the most part unseen, yet on their urge and energy life itself depends: without them living beings would be as inert as stones. But were they left to function unchecked, life would lose its meaning, being reduced once more to mere

---

* In differing ways, Groddeck,[90] Reich,[91] Marcuse,[92] and N. O. Brown[93] show the interesting results of being more Freudian than Freud, of going the whole way and trusting the id. Groddeck's work seems to have fallen into obscurity, and it is strange that Brown does not mention him.

birth and death, as in the teeming world of primordial swamps.[94]

We are never allowed to forget, in the Jungian philosophy, that not only consciousness but also psychic integration, the goal of therapy, is *precarious*. It echoes the Biblical warning, "Brethren be sober, be vigilant, for your adversary the Devil walketh about as a roaring lion, seeking whom he may devour." The unconscious can be creative, it seems, only if skillfully pacified by the conscious, which must act all the while like the wary trainer of a performing lion. Therefore unless the lion is first tamed, the "invasion" of the conscious by unconscious contents which is said to occur in mystical experience will unleash the demons instead of the gods.

The conception of man as an angel riding a wild animal is also basic to the anthropological theories which arose out of Darwin's doctrine of evolution by natural selection. Consciousness and reason are precarious because they are the fragile "epiphenomena" of the blind and bestial process of physical evolution. They are the freakish products of the famous "primordial swamp," so freakish that there is really no common measure between the two. Outside man's skin there is really nothing corresponding to the intelligence inside it. Our survival must therefore be the cautious and rigidly controlled exploitation of a natural fluke. At the same time, anthropologists made an equation between primordial and near-animal man, on the one hand, with the child and the primitive, on the other. Was it altogether by chance that "primitives" turned out to be just those peoples upon whom the Western Europeans wanted to confer the benefits of their more "evolved" civilization?

In the nineteenth century our actual information about early man was negligible; our position is not much better even now. But, in differing ways, both Freud and Jung constructed a theory of primordial man for which there is no historical evidence. Its assumptions are: (1) that intelligence rests precariously on a biological and instinctual basis which is "animal" in the worst sense; (2) that existing cultures differing from ours in not having developed certain scientific and literary skills are survivals of primordial man, and are thus dubbed "primitive"; and (3) that by analogy with the repetition of evolutionary changes in the growth of the human fetus, the first years of infancy rehearse man's primordial mentality.[95] Take these assumptions hand in hand with the fact that psychotherapy was at first preoccupied with the study of deranged personalities, and what happens? It is assumed that irrational behavior is *historical* regression, that the disturbed individual is having difficulty in coping with traits which he inherits from the primordial swamp. In other words, what is repressed in the unconscious is the historical and prehistorical past, and consequently psychoanalysis becomes a tool for investigating the earliest history of man. In default of real evidence about primordial man, such a theory can only be self-validating.

All this has been said before, by others. I raise it here because it is the basis of Jung's theory of the evolution of consciousness and the ego. It leads him to regard the egocentric mode of consciousness as a universal and historically necessary step in the development of mankind. It is the problematic but essential mechanism for regulating the primordial instincts of the swamp and the cave, for raising mankind from the merely animal level. But we should consider another alternative: that man's peculiar bestiality has little to do with beasts; that his irrationalities, inordinate appetites, mass hysterias, and deeds of shocking violence and cruelty are not historically regressive at all; they are protests against just this mode of consciousness, against the double-bind of a self-contradictory social institution. Does not the practice, as distinct from the theory, of psychotherapy confirm this again and again? The disturbed individual is not so much the historical throwback in whom sufficient ego strength somehow failed to develop; he is the victim of too much ego, too much individual isolation. Furthermore, one should not assume that the development of an ego is the universally necessary basis for consciousness and intelligence. The neural structures of that "enchanted loom," the brain, upon which intelligence depends, are certainly not the deliberate creations of any conscious ego, and they do not dissolve into pulp when the ego is seen to be fictitious — by an act of intelligence. It would follow, then, that when the ego is dispelled there is not an "invasion" of consciousness by primordial contents from the swamp and the jungle. There is, instead, insight: the perception of a whole new pattern of relationships comparable to scientific or artistic discovery.

Jung has often been accused of "psychologism," but I am not, like Buber, using this word to criticize his neglect of the metaphysical or supernatural grounds of spiritual experience. The point is rather that his view of the "unconscious" on the one hand and of the content of the liberation experience on the other is too narrowly psychological. Of course, one can say that all experience is psychological experience because it happens in the psyche. But aside from the question of whether there really is a psyche, doesn't the equation of all experience with psychological experience make the latter term meaningless? As we have seen, the unconscious, which needs to be examined for man's liberation, contains physical, biological, and social relationships which are repressed not so much by a "psychological organ," such as the ego, as by defective communication and language. Nor is the content of the liberation experience — *satori, Nirvana,* "cosmic consciousness," etc. — something psychological in the sense of a flash of subjective light.[*] Its content is the physical world, seen in a new way.

> While Rikko, a high government official of the T'ang dynasty, had a talk with his Zen master Nansen, the official quoted a saying of Sojo, a noted monk-scholar of an earlier dynasty:
>
> > *Heaven and earth and I are of the same root,*
> > *The ten-thousand things and I are of one substance,*
>
> and continued, "Is not this a most remarkable statement?"
> Nansen called the attention of the visitor to the flowering plant in the garden and said, "People of the world look at these flowers as if they were in a dream."[97]

The event of seeing the world in a new way is perhaps psychological in that it is an event of perception and intelligence. But its content is not psychological in the sense of an "archetype" or visionary form seen in a dream or trance. When Nansen pointed to the flowers, he was not using them as a symbol of something psychological. If anything, he was pointing away

---

[*]   I have discussed the "subjective phenomena" of this experience elsewhere,[96] showing that they are quite incidental to its content — like the feeling of relief that comes with solving a difficult problem.

from the psychological, from the private and enclosed world of
the "subject." He was pointing at the flowers.

Considering the general character of Western assumptions
about Buddhism and Taoism — according to which they are religions — Jung is hardly to be blamed for a wrong classification
of the domain in which their experiences happen. We think of religious and spiritual experiences as events of the "inner life," but
this is all because of the false severance of the subject from the
object. The Eastern ways direct their students to "look within,"
to find out the self, only to dispel the illusion that it is inside as
distinct from outside. As the Chinese Zen master Lin-chi put it:
"Make no mistake: there is nothing on the outside and, likewise,
nothing on the inside that you can grasp."[98]

We cannot leave Freud and Jung, the great masters of
"depth psychology," without asking whether there is any connection between liberation and the analysis of dreams, as well
as the whole process of free association. Psychotherapists are
often surprised to find that the ways of liberation seem almost
entirely unconcerned with dreams, and this is just because their
orientation is not exactly psychological in our sense. It is sometimes assumed that liberation is a work to be undertaken only by
those who have gone beyond the need for anything that dream
analysis can achieve, but this would be to put it on too remote
a pedestal. My own hypothesis is that dream analysis is a "gim-
mick" (*upaya*), useful in therapy but not essential to it. Free association, or unblocked communication, is more fundamental,
but this is a technique which can be related to matters other than
dreams — Rorschach pictures, stories, everyday events, lists of
words, and, indeed, almost anything. Its use will be discussed in
the next chapter.

The theory that dreams are important goes hand in hand

with the idea that the unconscious is primarily psychological and subjective, in which case dreams would seem to be the royal road to finding out what goes on in the "hidden night life" of the patient. Needless to say, psychoanalysis has been much criticized for its tendency to speak of *the* unconscious as if it were a psychological organ with a mind of its own. The permanent value of Freud's hypothesis is in the way in which it directed attention to unconscious*ness*, to the fact that we are not aware of how we are conditioned to think and act as we do. L. L. Whyte[99] has suggested that it would be far more accurate to speak of man's life as "unconscious process with conscious aspects," and obviously "unconscious process" in this sense goes far beyond the psychological domain. "Unconsciousness" would correspond exactly with the Buddhist term *avidya* (ignore-ance), but there is no real equivalent of the "unconscious" in Indian or Chinese terms.*

To some extent the postulates of Existential analysis are more consistent with the ways of liberation than are those of either Freud or Jung. Rollo May[100] explains that this movement has arisen out of the dissatisfaction of many psychiatrists with such traditional concepts as the libido, the censor, the unconscious, and indeed the whole psychoanalytical theory of man. In particular Ludwig Binswanger, one of its main exponents, attacks "the cancer of all psychology up to now...the cancer of the doctrine of subject-object cleavage of the world."[101] Man is an "I am" not as a detached ego but as *being-in-the-world*, with emphasis on

---

* The nearest equivalent is perhaps the Mahayana Buddhist expression *alaya-vijnana*, or "store consciousness," which really designates the totality of *samskaras* or habitual patterns of psychophysical activity. The common criticism, often made by Coomaraswamy and others, that Western psychologists fail to distinguish between the subconscious and the superconscious does not seem very helpful. There would be some point in making a contrast between unconsciousness and expanded consciousness.

the dynamic, process character of *being* and on the fact that this *being* is necessarily in relation to a world. The world with which every subject is polarized is threefold: the *Umwelt* of our biological and physical foundations, the *Mitwelt* of social relations, and the *Eigenwelt* of one's own inner life and self-consciousness. No therapy can be adequate which does not take account of all three realms of relation. May[102] notes that the likeness between Existential analysis and such Eastern philosophies as Taoism and Zen goes

> ...much deeper than the chance similarity of words. Both are concerned with ontology, the study of being. Both seek a relation to reality which cuts below the cleavage between subject and object. Both would insist that the Western absorption in conquering and gaining power over nature has resulted not only in the estrangement of man from nature but also indirectly in estrangement of man from himself. The basic reason for these similarities is that Eastern thought never suffered the radical split between subject and object that has characterized Western thought, and this dichotomy is exactly what existentialism seeks to overcome.

So far so good. But we have seen that the Existential school takes anxiety, Kierkegaard's *angst*, and its concomitant guilt as inseparable from *being*, since "to be" implies "not to be," and since to know fully that one exists will necessarily involve the dread of not existing. Perhaps this is a therapeutic gambit, for one is a great deal less anxious if one feels perfectly free to be anxious, and the same may be said of guilt. Or it may be that there would be no joy in being alive save in relation to the awesome prospect of death. Yet the Existentialists give, rather, the impression that to live without anxiety is to live without seriousness. Being and nonbeing are not so much a polarity as a "dialectic of crisis," an oscillation, a wobbling on the brink, which is precisely Kierkegaard's "fear and trembling."* Not to be thus anxious, not to take one's own and other people's being-in-the-world seriously, is to disregard the whole dignity of being a person, to fail in being fully human.

Here we run straight into an ancient quarrel between West and East, since the former has always alleged that the latter does not take human personality seriously. Slavery, downtrodden women, starvation, a million dead of cholera — such is life! Is not this the Buddhist formula *sarva samskara duhkha, sarva samskara anatma, sarva samskara anitya*, all compounds (including people) are in anguish, all compounds are without self, all compounds are impermanent? If this be true, does it not make liberation the art of learning not to care? The stereotyped attitudes of a culture are, of course, always a parody of the insights of its more gifted members. Not caring is the parody of serenity, just as worrying is the parody of concern. We shall gain more understanding if we compare East and West at a higher level, and the comparison is often best as projected into superb works of art. Thus if we compare the faces of Christ and the Madonna of Michelangelo's Pietà in St. Peter's, Rome, with that astonishing statue of the Buddha-to-come, Maitreya, at Horyu-ji in Nara, what do we find? Anxiety? Anguish? On the contrary,

---

* Gregory Bateson[103] has explored, at least tentatively, the possibility of a connection between such oscillatory emotional states as anxiety (trembling), sobbing, and laughing and life situations in which there is a logical paradox. An electric bell oscillates because its armature is so arranged that when the current is turned on, it switches itself off, but this in turn switches it on. Yes implies No, and No implies Yes. He points out a similar property in the statement "I am lying," which is false if true, etc., and in the whole mechanism of the double-bind. But if this goes right to the root of life, should we tremble or laugh?

there is in all three faces an incredible mixture of tenderness, wise sadness, serene — and somehow utterly confident — resignation, all with the slightest hint of a smile. Each face is young and unwrinkled and yet immeasurably old — in the sense that these are the faces of immortal archetypes who have seen everything, understood everything, and endured everything without the least bitterness, at one extreme, or sentimentality, at the other. None are without concern or sorrow, and yet there is not the faintest trace of guilt or apprehension.

Are the attitudes expressed on these divine faces humanly possible? This is, as a matter of fact, the face that many people wear in death and which accounts for the extraordinary nobility of so many death masks. Here, of course, we are all out of our depth and there is nothing in the way of statistics or scientific information to help us. But I think I may hazard the suggestion that in the moment of death many people undergo the curious sensation not only of accepting but also of having willed everything that has happened to them. This is not willing in the imperious sense; it is the unexpected discovery of an identity between the willed and the inevitable.

It is to this that the recognition of the inseparability of being and nonbeing should lead us. This is the whole meaning of polarity, of life implying death, of subject implying object, of man implying world, and of Yes implying No. The ways of liberation propose that what many, perhaps, discover in death may also be discovered in the midst of life. Just as liberation involves the recognition of oneself in what is most other, it involves the recognition of life in death — and this is why so many rites of initiation take the neophyte through a symbolic death. He accepts the certainty of death so completely that, in effect, he is dead already — and thus beyond anxiety. In the words of the Zen master Bunan:

While living, be a dead man, thoroughly dead;
Whatever you do, then, as you will, is always good.[104]

This is where Freud and Jung seem in some ways to be wiser than the Existentialists: they see that death is the goal of life. Nonbeing fulfills being; it does not negate being, just as space does not negate what is solid. Each is the condition for the reality of the other. This is why Norman Brown is so right in saying that it is just death which gives the organism its individual uniqueness.

> The precious ontological uniqueness which the human individual claims is conferred on him not by possession of an immortal soul but by possession of a mortal body.... At the simplest organic level, any particular animal or plant has uniqueness and individuality because it lives its own life and no other — that is to say, because it dies.... If death gives life individuality and if man is the organism which represses death, then man is the organism which represses his own individuality. Then our proud views of humanity as a species endowed with an individuality denied to lower animals turns out to be wrong. The lilies of the field have it because they take no thought of the morrow, and we do not. Lower organisms live the life proper to their species; their individuality consists in their being concrete embodiments of the essence of their species in a particular life which ends in death.[105]

Thus the Existentialists are right in saying that nonbeing and death give being, a being, its authenticity. But anxiety is the repression of death, for whatever is repressed does not simply vanish from sight; it lurks in the corner of one's eye as a perpetual distraction, and the center of vision and attention trembles because it cannot fully look away from it. If at the popular, parodied level the East has no concern for the person, it is not because of liberation; it is because of the popular doctrine of re-incarnation, which implies that the individual, the ego, is unable to die. To be released from reincarnation is to be able to die, and thus to be able to live.

> The Nirvana-principle [says Norman Brown, using the term, unlike Freud, in its proper sense] regulates an individual life which enjoys full satisfaction and concretely embodies the full essence of the species, and in which life and death are simultaneously affirmed, because life and death together constitute individuality, and ripeness is all.[106]

What amounts in Existentialism to an idealization of anxiety is surely no more than a survival of the Protestant notion that it is *good* to feel guilty, anxious, and serious. This is quite a different matter from admitting honestly that that is how one feels, thereby breaking the vicious circle of anxiety by ceasing to be anxious about being anxious. Allowed anxiety ceases to be anxiety, for the whole nature of anxiety is that it *is* a vicious circle. It is the frustration of not being able to have life without death, that is, of not being able to solve a nonsensical problem. As Freud saw, the ego is constituted by a repression of Eros and Thanatos, of life and death, and for this reason it is a parody of authentic individuality. And as Norman Brown goes on to show, repressed Thanatos turns itself outward as the desire to kill, as aggression; and, on the other hand, repressed Eros becomes a fixation to the past, to the search for satisfaction in the repetition of some primary experience of satisfaction.

> Under conditions of repression, the repetition-compulsion establishes a fixation to the past, which alienates the neurotic from the present and commits him to the unconscious quest for the past in the future.[107]

It is thus that the Western equivalent of reincarnation is our obsession with history, "a forward-moving *recherche du temps perdu*,"[108] the fruitless attempt to move forward to a satisfactory future by the logic of an impoverished past. For history is the record of frustration, and its earliest sources are the monuments in which men began, in Unamuno's phrase, to store up their dead. History is the refusal to "let the dead bury their dead." History, or better, historicism, is a chronic hoarding of trash in the hope that it will someday "come in useful." It is the state of mind in which the record of what is done becomes more important than what is done, in which there is less and less room for action because of more and more room given over to results. This is why the *Bhagavadgita* describes liberation as action without clinging to the fruits of action, for when life and death are lived completely they proceed without trace in an eternal present.

Life is renewed by death because it is again and again set free from what would otherwise become an insufferable burden of memory and monotony. Genuine reincarnation lies in the fact that whenever a child is born "I" — or human awareness — arises into the world again with memory wiped clean and the wonder of life restored. Everlasting annihilation is as nonsensical as everlasting individuality. And who can doubt that if human life has arisen in this tiny area of one immense galaxy, it must be happening again and again, on grounds of sheer probability, throughout the whole diffusion of nebulae that surrounds us? For where the organism is intelligent the environment also must be intelligent.

Like so much of our psychotherapy, Existentialism does not actually take full account of death. Indeed, in the whole literature of psychotherapy there is the barest mention of suitable treatment for the patient facing death, and this is not, I fear, from the recognition that the problem of death is not a problem at all. It is, rather, from the feeling that it is an *insoluble* problem, a hard, inevitable fact which is "just too bad." Yet, again, the Existentialists are on the right track. If death makes the individual authentic, the authentic psychotherapy will be the first one to take death in its stride. When a patient is about to die, or is struck in mid-life with the dread of death, this is not the moment to hand him over to the *consoling* ministrations of some religious fantast who will try to explain death away. No one, I believe, has made any serious and rigorous study of the degree to which the fear of death is involved in the psychoses and neuroses. To ignore it or explain it away is to pass up the major opportunity of psychotherapy, for what death negates is not the individual, not the organism/environment, but the ego, and therefore liberation from the ego is synonymous with the full acceptance of death. For the ego is not a vital function of the organism; it is abstracted by social influence from memories; it is the hypothetical substance upon which memory is recorded, the constant which endures through all the changes of experience. To identify with the ego is to confuse the organism with its history, to make its guiding principle a narrowly selected and incomplete record of what it has been and done. This abstraction from memory thereupon seems to be a concrete and effective agent. But it is just this which is lost in death. Oneself as a *story* comes to an end, which shows that the ego is in every sense a story.

Apart from Existentialism, it seems to me that one of the most fruitful approaches to psychotherapy must lie among the lines begun by H. S. Sullivan and Frieda Fromm-Reichmann, for it is here that the social context of personality begins to be taken with full seriousness, and, as Sullivan himself said, the self-system (ego) as we know it today is "the principal stumbling block to favorable changes in personality."[109]

> The general science of psychiatry seems to me to cover much the same field as that which is studied by social psychology, because scientific psychiatry has to be defined as the study of interpersonal relations, and this in the end calls for the use of the kind of conceptual framework that we now call *field theory*. From such a standpoint, personality is taken to be hypothetical. That which can be studied is the pattern of processes which characterize the interaction of personalities in particular recurrent situations or fields which "include" the observer.[110]

On one side, this line of thought has spread out into the whole work of the Washington School with its highly intelligent interest in the ways of liberation, and, on another, to the study of psychotherapy as a problem of communication, "the social matrix of psychiatry," as explored in varying ways by Jurgen Ruesch,[111] Gregory Bateson,[112] Anatol Rapoport,[113] Jay Haley,[114] and others. This latter development seems to be gaining rather slow recognition, especially in Europe, because of the false impression that it represents a complete dehumanization of psychiatry in which man is studied by analogy with electronic computers and systems of mathematical logic. Yet it is just from here that we get such a concept as the double-bind, which, quite apart from its merits in identifying the causes of schizophrenia, may well prove to be one of the very great ideas in the whole history of psychology.

After all, if mathematical thinking has given us such deep understanding of physics and astronomy without in any way destroying the glory of the stars, why should it not someday prove as useful in understanding ourselves without in any way destroying the dignity of man? In any case, mathematics has long ceased to mean mere mechanics, and what is feared is that a mathematical description of man's behavior will reduce him to a machine without poetry. It is a serious mistake to oppose poetry to mathematics as the living flesh to the driest bones. The problem is merely that mathematics as taught begins in the arid wastes of arithmetic, elementary algebra, and Euclid — screening out poets from the start. The living flesh is substance and stuff only to those whose eyes are so dull that they cannot see the beauty of its patterns. Taken to its full possibilities, mathematical thinking can reveal the physical world to be something astonishingly akin to music.

It is feared, too, that when methods of this kind are pursued too far in the study of man and of his world, all their sublime unities may be disintegrated into digital, discontinuous bits, and that, again, the "human image" may vanish into more arrangements of point units. Those who think mathematically and analytically have gone some way in this direction, but this is why they are the first to discover its limits. In the words of Jurgen Ruesch:

> The peculiarities of language introduce a number of distortions into psychiatric research. When words are employed to refer to behavior action and movement, which are continuous functions, are sliced into discrete elements, as if they were replaceable parts of a machine. The continuity of existence thus is split into arbitrary entities which are not so much a function of actual behavior as the result of language structure."[5]

And while I know of no one who has thought more analytically and mathematically of human behavior than Gregory Bateson, he has this to say:

The old Berkeleyan motto, *esse est percipi* — to be is to be perceived — leads on the one hand to such philosophical toys as the question, Is the tree there in the wood when I am not there to see it? But on the other hand it leads to a very profound and irresistible discovery that the laws and processes of our perception are a bridge which joins us inseparably to that which we perceive — a bridge which unites subject and object.... To increase awareness of one's scientific universe is to face unpredictable increases in one's awareness of the self. And I wish to stress the fact that such increases are always in the very nature of the case unpredictable in nature.... No one knows the end of that process which starts from uniting the perceiver and the perceived — the subject and the object — into a single universe.[116]

To lose the reality of the isolated ego is not, as Erich Fromm[117] seems to fear, to lose the integrity of the individual.* To find that the organism is inseparable from its environment is neither to lose the clarity of its form nor the uniqueness of its position. Furthermore, to remove the particular type of repression which ego-consciousness involves is not to throw the gates open to the unrestrained rapacity of the id. For it is not the ego which makes man different from serpents, lions, sharks, and apes; it is his organic structure, and the type of environment in which this structure can appear. It is not romantic and sentimental to blame the peculiar violence and cruelty of man upon social institutions rather than on nature. It is true that men have invented these

---

* Fromm's disagreements with Sullivan as to the reality of the "self" are surely based on the semantic confusion whereby the terms "I," "ego," "self," "person," "individual," etc., are used indiscriminately and interchangeably. Were it otherwise, Fromm's deep interest in Zen Buddhism[118] would be inconceivable.

institutions, but is it not obvious that what may start out as a small and unnoticed mistake may turn into a catastrophe as one rolling pebble may start an avalanche? Who could have known that the mistake of regarding men as separate egos would have had such disastrous consequences? But it is easy to be wise in retrospect.

As the Chinese Taoists have seen, there is really no alternative to trusting man's nature. This is not wishful thinking or sentimentality; it is the most practical of practical politics. For every system of mistrust and authoritarian control is *also* human. The will of the would-be saint can be as corrupt as his passions, and the intellect can be as misguided as the instincts. The authority and effectiveness of the police are only as sound as public morale. Faith in our own nature works if it works only fifty-one percent of the time. The alternative, as Freud saw, is the swelling of guilt "to a magnitude that individuals can hardly support."

V. The Countergame

The social psychologist is always in danger of being a deter-
minist, seeing individual behavior as subordinate to social
behavior, the organism as responding willy-nilly to the conditions of its environment. If we define the organism by a complex
boundary — the external skin, the skins of internal organs as
well, down to the very surfaces of cells and molecules — its behavior will consist in the movements of this boundary. But the
boundary of the organism is *also* the boundary of its environment, and thus its movements can be ascribed to the environment as well. Systems of description ascribe these movements
now to one side and now to the other, and these changes of
viewpoint are mutually corrective. Philosophical fashions swing
between voluntarism and determinism, idealism and positiv-
ism, realism and nominalism, and there is never any clear issue
between these alternatives when one regards them as opposed.
The point I have been trying to make all along is that we gain

better understanding by describing this boundary and its movements as belonging to both the organism and its environment,
but that we do not ascribe the origin of movement to either side.
The question as to which side of a curved surface moves first
is always unanswerable, unless we restrict our observations to
limited areas and ignore some of the factors involved.

We have seen that the social game is based on conventional
rules, and that these define the significant areas to be observed
and the ways in which the origin of action is to be ascribed to one
side of the boundary or another. Thus all social games regard
the boundary between organism and environment, the epider-
mis, as significant, and almost all regard the inside of this boundary as an independent source of action. They tend to ignore the
fact that its movements can also be ascribed to the environment,
but this "ignore-ance" is one of the rules of the game. But when
the philosopher, the psychologist, or the psychiatrist begins to
observe human behavior more carefully, he starts to question the
rules and to notice the discrepancies between social definitions
and physical events. To quote Bateson again:

> There seems to be a sort of progress in awareness, through
> the stages of which every man — and especially every
> psychiatrist and every patient — must move, some per-
> sons progressing further through these stages than others.
> One starts by blaming the identified patient for his idio-
> syncrasies and symptoms. Then one discovers that these
> symptoms are a response to — or an effect of — what
> others have done; and the blame shifts from the identi-
> fied patient to the etiological figure. Then, one discovers
> perhaps that these figures feel a guilt for the pain which
> they have caused, and one realizes that when they claim
> this guilt they are identifying themselves with God. After

all, they did not, in general, know what they were doing, and to claim guilt for their acts would be to claim omniscience. At this point one reaches a more general anger, that what happens to people should not happen to dogs, and that what people do to each other the lower animals could never devise. Beyond this, there is, I think, a stage which I can only dimly envisage, where pessimism and anger are replaced by something else — perhaps humility. And from this stage onward to whatever other stages there may be, there is loneliness.[119]

This is the loneliness of liberation, of no longer finding security by taking sides with the crowd, of no longer believing that the rules of the game are the laws of nature. It is thus that transcending the ego leads to great individuality.

Who, then, wants to follow this path? Liberation begins from the point where anxiety or guilt becomes insupportable, where the individual feels that he can no longer tolerate his situation as an ego in opposition to an alien society, to a universe in which pain and death deny him, or to negative emotions which overwhelm him. Ordinarily, he is quite unaware of the fact that his distress arises from a contradiction in the rules of the social game. He blames God, or other people, or even himself — but none of these are responsible. There has simply been a mistake, whose consequences no one could have foreseen — a wrong step in biological adaptation which, presumably, seemed at first to be very promising. L. L. Whyte,[120] in his marvelous account of the way in which the duality of the human nervous system became the conflicting dualism of reason against instinct, writes:

> Intellectual man had no choice but to follow the path which facilitated the development of his faculty of thought, and

thought could only clarify itself by separating out static
concepts which, in becoming static, ceased to conform
to their organic matrix or to the forms of nature.... Eu-
ropean languages in general begin with a subject-noun
whose action is expressed in an active verb. Some apparently permanent element is separated from the general
process, treated as an entity, and endowed with active responsibility for a given occurrence. This procedure is so
paradoxical that only long acquaintance with it conceals
its absurdity.

It is thus, then, that the ego is separated out as the static entity
responsible for action, and from this mistake the trouble begins.

In quest of liberation from this problem the individual
therefore goes to the *guru* or to the psychotherapist with such
questions as: "How can *I* escape from birth-and-death (*samsara*)?" "What shall *I do* to be saved?" "How can *I* get out of
these extreme depressions?" "How can *I* stop *myself* drinking
so much?" "I am terrified of getting cancer, and how am *I* to
stop worrying?" All these questions take as real the very illusion which constitutes the actual problem, but what is the *guru*
or therapist to do? He cannot say, "Stop worrying," because
the ego is not in control, and just that seems to be the problem.
He cannot say, "Accept your fears," without implying that the
ego is an effective agent which can actively accept. He cannot
say, "There's nothing you can do about it," without leaving the
impression that the ego is the helpless victim of fate. He cannot say, "Your trouble is that you think you're an ego," because
the inquirer genuinely feels that he is, or, if he doubts it, will
come back with the question: "Well, how am *I* to stop thinking
so?" There is no direct answer to an irrational question, which
was why one Zen master replied, none too helpfully, "When

you know the answer you won't ask the question!" As we have seen, almost the only thing that the *guru* or therapist can do is to persuade the individual to act upon his false premise in certain consistent directions until he sees his mistake. To do this the individual must be drawn into a game, playing *as if* his ego were real, but not along the wandering or circular paths of ordinary life which do not involve the experiments necessary for the denouement. The *guru* therefore initiates a "countergame," a game countering the contradictions in the social game.

The genesis of this idea came to me from J. Haley's delightful and ostensibly satirical comparison of psychoanalysis with the "ploys" or techniques of the British humorist Stephen Potter for getting socially "one-up" on other people — the art of "One-upmanship."[121] I am afraid that Haley's article was none too well received by the many therapists who missed its point and felt themselves accused of conducting a very artful racket, or worse, of being therapists because of an unconscious need to be one-up on other people. I am sure Haley did not miss the humor of this misunderstanding, but his article was in fact intended as a serious contribution to psychoanalytic theory. I shall defer going into the details of Haley's view of psychoanalysis until later. It is enough to say here that if the neurotic or ego-ridden individual is one who insists upon being one-up on his own feelings or on life as a whole, the analyst engages him in a game of one-upmanship in which he cannot win. As the game proceeds, it becomes apparent that the patient's contest with the analyst is one and the same as his contest with life, or with the alienated aspects of his own feelings. The game ends with the insight that the patient could not win because the very premises of the game were absurd: he was trying to make the subject one-up on the object, the organism one-up on the environment, himself one-up on himself. He had failed to see that every explicit duality is an implicit unity. Haley came to this clarification by trying to see whether psychoanalysis could be better understood by disregarding its theoretical postulates and simply describing what happens in analysis by way of communication and interpersonal exchange.

At first sight, Haley's hypothesis seems to be a tremendous oversimplification, and I was indeed inclined to this view until I began to try it out upon what I knew of the ways of liberation — to find that it was a simplification capable of almost endlessly complex expressions. The way of liberation to which Haley's view is most clearly applicable is Zen Buddhism, which, with Taoist humor, is regarded by its own masters as something of a racket. But the "ploys" of one-upmanship are just what the Zen masters refer to as their "old tricks," their "traps" for unwary students, or, in other words, the *upaya* — the "skillful means" which the compassionate bodhisattva employs to bring about the liberation of others.

The basic position of the Zen master is that he has nothing to teach, no doctrine, no method, no attainment or insight of any kind. In words attributed to the Buddha himself, "I obtained not the least thing from unexcelled, complete awakening, and for this very reason it is called 'unexcelled, complete awakening.'"[122] On one occasion a Zen master ascended the rostrum and gave a lecture consisting of total silence. When asked the meaning, he replied, "The scriptures are explained by the preachers, the commentaries by the commentators." What, then, does a Zen master explain? There is nothing to say because there is no problem. All that there is in Zen is said to be perfectly obvious from the beginning, and if there is anything to say at all it is just that "the water flows blue and the mountain towers green." This is not "beautiful" nature mysticism. When asked, "What is the Buddha?" another master replied, "Dried excrement!" Nor is it pantheism; it is no "ism" or doctrine of any kind. When asked, "What is the Way [Tao]?" Nansen answered, "Your everyday mind is the Way." "How, then, does one get into accord with it?" "If you try to accord, you deviate." Life, he is saying, is not a problem, so why are you asking for a solution?

Nevertheless, Zen is a discipline and a rugged one. Though there is nothing to teach, its masters accept students and establish seminaries for their training. Yet all this, said Lin-chi, "is like using an empty fist or yellow leaves to beguile a little child.* How can you find any juice from thorns and dried branches? There is nothing to be grasped outside the mind [everyday consciousness], and nothing inside. What is it that you seek? You say on all sides that the Tao is to be practiced and put to the proof. Do not be mistaken! If there is anyone who can practice it, he is just involving himself in *samsara*."[123] Or again, "It is said everywhere that there is a Way which must be followed and a method which must be practiced. What method do you say must be practiced, and what Way followed? What do you lack in what you are using right now? What will you add to where you are? Not understanding this, raw young students put faith in the spells of some wild fox, promising to help them attain liberation by some strange doctrine which just puts people in bondage."[124] Ma-tsu, an early master of the Tang dynasty, put the problem succinctly as follows:

> The Tao has nothing to do with discipline. If you say that
> it is attained by discipline, finishing the discipline turns out

---

* The child is crying for gold and thus is beguiled with yellow leaves.

to be losing the Tao....If you say there is no discipline, this is to be the same as ordinary [unliberated] people.[125]

But just because the Zen masters are so devastatingly frank, no one believes them. They do not appear to have any problem that seriously troubles them. The would-be student, however, has — and is therefore convinced that there must be some way, some method, of becoming as much at peace with the world and with oneself as the masters. For the masters seem to take the world and its sufferings as if it were just a dream, and the aspirant to Zen imagines that *he* could feel that way too if only he could find the right method for transforming his consciousness. Yet it is not possible to be accepted for Zen training without considerable persistence; all kinds of barriers are put in the applicant's way, but the more the barriers, the more his eagerness, the more he becomes sure that the master is guarding some deeply occult secret and testing his fitness and sincerity for admission to an elite. But by these means the assertion that he has a problem is put squarely on the applicant's own shoulders. As we say, "Anyone who goes to a psychiatrist ought to have his head examined!" In other words, his problem is his question, his belief that the question he is asking makes sense.

When at last the applicant gains admission to the master, he finds himself confronted by a very formidable figure — usually a much older man, superbly self-confident and at ease, completely present and undistracted, and with the kind of twinkle in his eyes which indicates that he sees through the student like glass. In Chinese and Japanese culture the Zen master is, furthermore, a great authority figure, far more so than father or grandfather, and the student meets with him in the most formal circumstances — the master enthroned in his inner sanctum, and the student bowing most humbly before him. Everything is done, in short, to impress the student that in being admitted he has received the greatest condescension from a personage who has attained heights of wisdom far beyond his ken. This is no mere pretense; or rather, it is very great mastery of a certain kind of bluff in which the master has the same confidence as a highly accomplished player of poker or chess.

Having, then, indicated his great earnestness to attain "awakening," the liberation which Zen promises, the student is given a *koan* or Zen question and told to return sometime later with an answer. The preliminary *koan* is in fact a concealed form of the question which the student has asked the master, "How can *I* attain liberation?" Though worded in many different ways, the *koan* is actually asking, "Who asks the question? Who wants to be liberated?" But the student is told that a merely verbal answer is not enough; he must *demonstrate* or in some way actually show this "who" in action. The master is saying, in effect, "You say *you* want to be liberated. Show me this *you!*" What this amounts to is a request for completely unpremeditated or spontaneous action which is also entirely sincere, but in circumstances so powerfully suggestive of the authority of his culture, this is about the last thing that a Chinese or Japanese student can do. By such means the student is, as we say in current slang, totally "bugged." How, in such formal circumstances, can he do something without first intending to do it? How can he conceal his prior intention from such an apparent mind reader? The formality of presenting an answer to the *koan* involves much preliminary ritual, and when he is finally seated before the master the student has to repeat the *koan* and then present his answer. The more he tries to be sincere and spontaneous, the more he is aware of contriving an answer. It is like being told that a wish will come true if you make it without thinking of a green elephant.

But this is not all. Between his interviews with the master the Zen student spends many hours in meditation, sitting cross-legged with his fellow students in the *ʒendo* or "meditation hall," watched by alert monks with "warning sticks" to beat the backs of those who fall asleep or go into a trance. Meditation in Zen is, first, an attempt to attain perfect concentration and control of thought by counting one's breaths, and, second, a period for devoting one's whole attention to the *koan* in quest of a solution. Students are urged to devote their minds exclusively to the *koan*, holding its question before them with all their energy, but looking at it rather than thinking about it since the solution is not to be found in an intellectual answer.

Looking at this "from the outside," we can see that the master has "tricked" the student into putting himself, voluntarily, into an extreme double-bind. In the first place, he is asked to show his naked and genuine self in the presence of one who represents the full authority of the culture, and who is felt to be the most acute judge of character. In the second place, he is asked to be spontaneous in circumstances where he can hardly be anything but deliberate. In the third place, he is asked to concentrate on something without thinking about it. In the fourth place, he cannot comment on the bind, not only because thinking about the *koan* is not the answer but also because the master will, even forcibly, reject all verbal comments. In the fifth place, he is not allowed to escape the dilemma by going into a trance. And all this calls for the most powerful exertion of his will or ego, though he is free at any time to quit the field.

In a wonderfully concealed way, the master has encouraged the student to commit himself to the solution of a self-contradictory problem (e.g., the *koan* "What is the sound of one hand?"). The student comes to feel that he *must* find the answer, but he is at the same time made to realize that there is no way of finding it — because everything that *he does* acting, as he thinks, as an ego is rejected as wrong. The *koan* can be answered, but you — the ego — must not answer it. You — the ego — must first meditate to get rid of the ego. As Eugen Herrigel discovered when studying with a Zen archery master, he was expected to release the bowstring without doing it himself, on purpose.[126] But let us remember that the self-contradictory problem to which all the student's energies are directed is the *same* problem which he originally brought to the master, which he went out of his way to insist upon and raise: How can my ego liberate itself? By asking this question the student engages himself in a game with the master in which the student can never win; he can never get one-up on the master because he can never get one-up on himself. The one hand cannot clap itself.

The individual has therefore been engaged in an intense struggle in which all his energy — misconceived as his ego strength — has been defeated. It seems that absolutely nothing that he can do is right, spontaneous, or genuine; he can act neither independently (self-fully) nor unselfishly. But in the moment of defeat he sees what this means: that he, the agent, cannot act, does not act, and never did act. There is just action — Tao. It is happening, but neither to anyone nor from anyone. At once, therefore, he ceases to block action by trying to make it (for there is no ego) do itself, force itself to be spontaneous, or right, or unselfish. Because, now, he has nothing to prove and nothing to lose; he can go back to the master and call his bluff.

Yet the ego is a very deeply ingrained habit of feeling, and such insights (*satori*), intense and convincing as they may be at the moment, have a way of wearing off. Knowing this, the master has many more tricks up his sleeve, and he says,

"Now you have reached a most important understanding, but as yet you have only entered the gate. To get the real understanding, you must practice still more diligently." This is, of course, a "come-on" to test the student and to see if he will fall for it, as, indeed, he will if there is still even the ghost of a notion that there is something in Zen to get. On the other hand, the student may go away, feeling no need for further study. But because the master has sown a doubt in his mind, it may not be long before he most apologetically returns, for so long as any doubt remains to be played upon, the job is not finished. In this way the game proceeds, ploy by ploy, until at last the student reaches the same unassailable position as the master's. For the master cannot lose the game because he does not care in the least whether he wins or loses. He has nothing to prove and nothing to defend.

Must this be taken to be true of his whole relation to life, and not just to the particular game of Zen, so that he actually does not care whether he lives or dies? In a way this is true, but only because he has not the least ambition to be courageous, and therefore puts up no resistance to his natural feelings. He does not create anxiety by trying to be one-up on anxiety. No aspect of experience, of emotion or feeling, remains alien — nor does he hold this state of affairs up to himself as an ideal. He has seen quite clearly that the idea of a controlling agent behind acts, thinker behind thoughts, and feeler behind feelings is an illusion. More correctly, it is seen not by him, but *in* the acting, thinking, and feeling.

It is, of course, one of the most familiar problems in psychotherapy that the free flow of a patient's thought or action is "blocked." In Zen this is called "doubt" or "hesitation" and is regarded as the chief symptom of ego, in contrast with "going directly ahead" (*mo chih ch'u*). Blocking is not thinking a problem out; it is *stopping* to think — a kind of anxious going blank through eagerness to win or fear to lose. Blocking is thus the typical response to a double-bind, and in the ordinary course of life it is the brief hesitation before thought or action which we confuse with an actual sensation of the ego. It is the feedback process, say, the cortex, trying to get feedback about itself and going blank because it is unable to do so. Thus part of the Zen master's game is to do everything possible to make the student block, until he ceases to care whether he blocks or not. This is well illustrated in the following incident:

> Nansen found the students of the eastern and western dormitories quarrelling over the ownership of a cat. Grasping hold of the cat, he exclaimed: "If anyone can say a true word, the cat can be saved!" There was no reply, whereupon Nansen immediately cut the cat in two. The same evening when Joshu returned, Nansen put the incident to him, and at once Joshu put his sandals on his head and walked out. "If only you had been here," said Nansen, "the cat could have been saved." [127]

The students blocked not only because they were stumped by such a sudden request for the "true word" about Zen but also because they were horrified at the thought of a Buddhist monk's slaying an animal. But nothing stopped Joshu. *

Westerners often ask whether it is absolutely necessary to go through such a disciplinary mill as Zen in order to attain liberation, or whether there might be some more efficient and less arduous way. The question really answers itself: the more you

---

* Zen anecdotes of this kind, called "question-answer" (*mondo*), could be cited indefinitely, and those interested in studying the actual performance of the game should consult Reps,[128] Suzuki,[129] and Watts.[130]

believe that liberation is something which *you* can get, the harder you will have to work. Liberation is attractive to the degree that one's ego seems to be a problem.

Another important example of the countergame is the Buddha's own dialectic of the "middle way," as it has recently been clarified by A. J. Bahm.[131] It appears that in the Buddha's own time and region of India the way of liberation was largely confused with an attempt to destroy the ego and its appetites by extreme measures of asceticism, which the Buddha himself tried and found useless. Instead, he proclaimed a middle way between asceticism and hedonism, but this was something much more than a counsel of moderation. The middle way is ultimately the implicit unity of contraries, something like Jung's "reconciling principle."

As always, the problem is posed by the aspirant, and here it is the desire to find release from anguish (*duhkha*). The Buddha's counter is that desire (*trishna*) is the cause of anguish, and so the dialectic continues:

A: Then how do I get rid of desire?

B: Do you really want to get rid of it?

A: Yes and no. I want to get rid of the desire that causes anguish; but I do not want to get rid of the desire to get rid of it.

B: Anguish consists in not getting what one desires. Therefore, do not desire more than you have or will be able to get.

A: But I shall still have anguish if I do not succeed in desiring only as much as I have or will get.

B: Do not then desire to succeed in any greater measure than you can or will.

A: But there is still anguish if I fail to accomplish *that*!

B: Do not then desire to accomplish more of *that* than you can or will.

A: Etc.

This is not a straight conversation. At every step the aspirant has been experimenting with the Buddha's advice, trying in meditation to discover the degree to which he can stop desire, desiring to stop desire, and so on. But notice that the design of the dialectic is not circular but convergent, and that each step is a meta-step with respect to the one before. On each higher level, the aspirant is learning to halve the distance between his excessive, and anguish-causing, desire and what can actually be done. In this manner he is being brought to accept things as they are, but, at each step, things as they are include more and more the way he feels about them, and the way he feels about his feelings, etc. As Bahm shows, the various steps correspond to the stages of meditation (*jhana*) described in the early Buddhist records.

> The *jhanas* may be interpreted as degrees of shifting from concern about means to enjoyment of ends. Each new increase in generality of acceptance entails an increase in what is included in that which is experienced as an end. *Jhanas* are degrees of freedom from anxiety. *Jhanas* constitute levels of clarification or enlightenment relative to the extensiveness of the generality embodied in present enjoyment. *Jhanas* are successive degrees of diminution of one's desire to interfere willfully in the natural course of events. *Jhanas* are shifts of interest increasingly from what ought to be to what is.[132]

In other words, as with each *jhana* stage the acceptance of what is includes more and more one's feelings about what is, there is going to come a point when the sphere of what is (the world) and the sphere of one's feeling or desire about it (the ego) are identical. The aspirant began by seeking release from anguish, from the world of birth-and-death (*samsara*) as a trap. But at the end there is *only* the trap, and thus no one caught in it!

Another form of the dialectic of the middle way in Buddhism is the celebrated Madhyamika system of Nagarjuna (cir. AD 200). At first sight this seems to be a purely philosophical and intellectual tour de force, the object of which is simply to refute any point of view that may be proposed. Taken in a purely logical and academic way, the Madhyamika is the systematic refutation of any philosophical opinion that may be classified under what Indian logic calls the "four propositions": (a) is, (b) is not, (c) both is and is not, and (d) neither is nor is not; or (a) being, (b) nonbeing, (c) both being and nonbeing, and (d) neither being nor nonbeing. Thus, for example, *a* would assert Being or Substance as the ultimate reality in the manner of St. Thomas Aquinas; *b* in Humean fashion would dismiss this as the mere reification of a concept; *c* in the synthetic style of Hegel would affirm both sides, stressing their mutuality; and *d* would be some form of agnosticism or nihilism. But because language is dualistic or relational, any affirmation or denial whatsoever can have meaning only in relation to its own opposite. Every statement, every definition, sets up a boundary or limit; it classifies something, and thus it can always be shown that what is inside the boundary must coexist with what is outside. Even the idea of the boundless is meaningless without the contrast of the bounded. The Madhyamika dialectic uses this as an infallible method for pointing out the relativity of any metaphysical premise, and thus to engage such a dialectician in argument is inevitably to play a losing game.

But the intention of the Madhyamika is not to create an infallible system for winning arguments. It is quite definitely a therapy, a liberative countergame, and it is one of the historical antecedents of the technique of Zen. Like the therapist or the Zen master, the Madhyamika dialectician makes no proposition and raises no problem. He waits for one to come to him, and, of course, the problem posed may not at first seem to be anything like a metaphysical proposition. The system assumes, however, that almost everyone, however unlearned, has some metaphysical premise, some usually unconscious opinion to which he clings very dearly, and which lies at the root of his psychological security. By careful questioning the dialectician finds out what this opinion is, and then he challenges the student to propose and defend it. Naturally, the defense fails and, to the degree that the student is emotionally dependent upon his opinion, he begins to feel insecure, not just intellectually but psychologically and even physically. He therefore looks about for some other premise to which he can hold, but as he takes up such alternatives the dialectician disposes of them one after another. At this point the student begins to feel a kind of vertigo because it seems that he has no basis from which to think and act, a situation which is obviously equivalent to the inability to find an ego agent. Because there is nowhere for him to take his stand there is also nowhere for him to be. Left to himself in this predicament he might well go out of his mind, but there is always the presence of the *guru* to reassure him, not by argument but by personality, that it is possible to have passed through this crisis with gain rather than loss of sanity. The "contest" of these countergames is always conducted under the supposition that the players are not equal, that the *guru* is the master, and that therefore this is a learning game rather than a real battle. This is presupposed by the student in the initial act of seeking the *guru*'s instruction.

Another form of the countergame, often used in Yoga and of which there is also a rather full account in connection with the Taoist sage Lieh-tzu,[133] centers around the task of attempting to gain perfect control of one's mind. The *guru* gives the student to understand that his problem lies not in the external world but in his own thoughts, feelings, and motivations. Pain and death will take care of themselves if only the student will take care of his own mind, and therefore he is encouraged to block his mental activity completely. At the same time, the student is given the impression that the *guru* can read his mind so that there is no chance of concealing its vagaries from the ever-watchful master.

This is an obvious double-bind, not only because the mind that needs to be controlled is the same as that which is trying to control it but also because the student is "bugged" and made painfully self-conscious by knowing that he is watched. The disadvantage of this method, accounting for the fact that Yoga is so often a cul-de-sac, is that it can easily degenerate into nothing more than a deep hypnotic trance. This is why the early Zen texts repeatedly discourage attempts to block mental activity completely, saying that if this be liberation, then blocks of wood and stone are already Buddhas.[134] However, the skillful *guru* will always lead the student's attempts at mind control into a vicious circle, reminding him, for example, that he is not really concentrating but thinking about trying to concentrate, or actually directing him to concentrate on concentration, to be aware of awareness, or urging him to concentrate upon some object without first, or subconsciously, intending to do so. The premise which the *guru* is challenging is the student's assumption that there really is a knower of his knowledge and a controller or thinker of his thoughts. While this assumption remains there is never perfect concentration because one is always "in two minds" — the knower and knowledge.

When at last the student discovers that "he" cannot really control his mind at all, and that however much he exerts himself his concentration is always "with intention," and that the *guru* knows it, he gives up and, in Lieh-tzu's words, "lets his mind think whatever it likes" — because there is simply no alternative. Whereupon he realizes that the mind is *always* concentrated; the thinker is always completely one with and absorbed in its thought because there is nothing else than the succession of thoughts!* Willing concentration merely introduces an oscillation effect into the succession of thoughts, because it is an attempt to make thought think itself. We can think about thinking by meta-thinking, by commenting on our thoughts at a higher level; but we cannot think thinking on one and the same level. When the confusion of this oscillation effect no longer arises, when, in other words, the yogi no longer tries to think with a thinker, his natural powers of concentration become enormously enhanced. There is no further "interference," in the electronic sense, from the supposed thinker.

A comparable technique is to encourage the student to stop his mind from wandering by thinking only about the events of the immediate present. Thought seems to be detached from time because memory images enable us to review events in succession and to project their future course. Because of this seeming ability to look now at the present, now at the past, and now at the future, the sensation of there being a constant thinker separate from the flow of events is all the more plausible. It therefore seems possible and reasonable to make an effort to attend to the present alone. But as the student perseveres, he discovers that

---

* Cf. the Zen master Ma-tsu: "A *sutra* says, 'It is only a group of elements which come together to make this body.' When it arises only these elements arise. When it ceases, only these elements cease. But when these elements arise, they do not say, 'I am arising,' and when they cease they do not say, 'I am ceasing.' So, too, with our former thoughts, later thoughts, and intervening thoughts: the thoughts follow one another without being linked together. Each one is absolutely tranquil."[135]

the actual present is astonishingly elusive. In the very micro-second that he observes a present event it has already become a memory image, and it seems that without time for events to impress themselves upon memory there is no way of knowing anything at all. But if knowing must involve this lapse of time, is not all knowledge knowledge of the past, and what we call present knowledge just knowledge of the immediate past? The task assigned appears to be impossible, for the present reduces itself to an infinitesimal nothing. Yet in the moment when the experiment fails it also succeeds, but in an unexpected way. For it strikes the student that the memory images themselves are present events, and, if this is so, there is no knowledge *except* knowledge of the present. He had therefore been tricked into trying to do what happens in any case. But now the illusion which made it possible for him to fall for the trick is dissolved: if all knowledge is knowledge of the present, there is no observer separate from the flow of events.

The common design of all these methods is now clear: they challenge the student to demonstrate the power and independence of his presumed ego, and to the extent that he believes this possible he falls into a trap. As the trap closes, his feeling of helplessness becomes more and more critical, just because his habitual sense of being able to act from his own center has been so completely challenged. While the least identification with the observing ego remains, he seems to be being reduced more and more to an inert and passive witness. His thoughts, feelings, and experiences appear to be a mutually conditioning series of events in which he cannot genuinely intervene, since it always turns out that intervention was motivated not by the ego, but by one or more of the observed events. Thoughts and feelings are conditioned by other thoughts and feelings, and the ego is cut down to a mute observer. Finally, as in the exercise of trying to concentrate only on the present, even its power to observe is challenged. Or perhaps its very passivity is challenged by the invitation to *be* passive, or simply to watch and accept what happens. But then, how is one to accept what happens when, among the things that are happening, there are feelings of resistance to life, of nonacceptance; or if it turns out that one is really accepting life in order to be one-up on it?

This is the point where, in the imagery of Zen, the student is likened to a mosquito biting an iron bull, or to a man who has swallowed a ball of red-hot iron which he can neither spit out nor gulp down. Press the point, and there is suddenly a "flip" of consciousness. There is no ego left with which one can identify. As a result the sense of self shifts from the independent observer to everything that is "observed." It feels that one *is* all that one knows, that one is doing all that is seen to happen, for the conflict of subject and object has entirely disappeared. This may at first be disconcerting and confusing, because there seems to be no independent point from which to act upon events and control them. It is like the moment in which one first learns to ride a bicycle or to swim: the new skill seems to be happening by itself. "Look, Mama, no hands!" But as the shock of unfamiliarity wears off, it becomes possible to conduct one's affairs in this new dimension of consciousness without the least difficulty.

In the language of psychotherapy, what we have here is the end of alienation, both of the individual from himself and of the individual from nature. The new state of affairs could also be described as self-acceptance or as psychological integration. However unscientific his terminology, and whatever his presuppositions about the biology of reason and instinct, this is certainly what Jung has in mind as the outcome of therapy.

One must be able to let things happen. I have learnt from
the East what is meant by the phrase *Wu-wei*: namely,
"not-doing, letting be," which is quite different from
doing nothing.... The region of darkness into which one
falls is not empty; it is the "lavishing mother" of Lao-tzu,
the "images" and the "seed." When the surface has been
cleared, things can grow out of the depths. People always
suppose that they have lost their way when they come
up against these depths of experience. But if they do not
know how to go on, the only answer, the only advice, that
makes any sense is "Wait for what the unconscious has
to say about the situation." A way is only *the* way when
one finds it and follows it oneself. There is no general pre-
scription for "how one should do it."[136]

"The region of darkness" and "the unconscious" are, of course,
this unfamiliar world of polarity where we live as organism/
environment instead of subject at war with alien objects, and
it is dark and unconscious only because it has been repressed
by our conventional way of seeing things. This is quite clearly,
too, the mode of consciousness which both Norman Brown and
Herbert Marcuse see as the logical outcome of psychoanalysis — if one follows it with a consistency which Freud himself
seemed to lack.

Freud describes the "ideational content" of the surviving
primary ego-feeling as "limitless extension and oneness
with the universe" (oceanic feeling)....He suggests that
the oceanic feeling seeks to reinstate "limitless narcissism."
The striking paradox that narcissism, usually understood
as egotistic withdrawal from reality, here is connected
with oneness with the universe, reveals the new depth
of the conception: beyond all immature autoeroticism,

narcissism denotes a fundamental relatedness to reality which may generate a comprehensive existential order. In other words, narcissism may contain the germ of a different reality principle: the libidinal cathexis of the ego (one's new body) may become the source and reservoir for a new libidinal cathexis of the objective world — transforming this world into a new mode of being.[137]

Wherever something of this kind emerges from the Freudian tradition, it is assumed that the new relationship of man to his world will be *erotic* — not the specialized eroticism of the genital apparatus, but the diffused eroticism of primary narcissism and of the "polymorphous perverse" body of the infant. Psychoanalysts of what I must call the hard-boiled variety regard all this dabbling with mysticism and oceanic feelings as pure regression, as an expression of the infant's global *egotism* which completely disregards any real problems of divergent interests between oneself and others. But narcissism is necessarily *egotism* only if it can be assumed that conflict between the organism and its environment is biologically prior to the mutual development of the two, and in the present state of our knowledge this simply cannot be maintained. In discussing man's "earliest encounters of his trustful past" in infancy, even so ego-oriented an analyst as Erik Erikson can say:

> Finally, the glass shows the pure self itself, the unborn core of creation, the — as it were, preparental — center where God is pure nothing: *ein lauter Nichts*, in the words of Angelus Silesius. God is so designated in many ways in Eastern mysticism. This pure self is the self no longer sick with a conflict between right and wrong, not dependent on providers, and not dependent on guides to reason and reality.... But must we call it regression if man thus

seeks again the earliest encounters of his trustful past in his efforts to reach a hoped-for and eternal future?...If this is partial regression, it is a regression which, in retracing firmly established pathways, returns to the present amplified and clarified.[138]

And earlier he has said:

From the oldest Zen poem to the most recent psychological formulation, it is clear that "the conflict between right and wrong is the sickness of the mind."[139]

In the stress upon the erotic and delightful character of this new feeling for the world, Westerners inclined to oriental mysticism will also demur out of the feeling that liberation is a purely "spiritual" condition. They join hands with Freud and the hard-boiled psychoanalysts in basic mistrust of the physical world, that is, in alienation from the organism, forgetting that when India and Tibet looked for the supreme symbol of the reconciliation of opposites they chose *shakta* and *shakti*, the god and the goddess, the figure and the ground, the Yes and the No, in eternal intercourse — using the most erotic image imaginable.

But I have tried to show that everything ascetic, spiritual, and other-worldly in the ways of liberation is a challenge to the ego — a come-on or judo inciting the student to prove that his central self is an independent soul agent which can make itself one-up on the world. The hard discipline of the ways is the total defeat of this ambition, leading to a new identification of one's life and being not with the encapsulated "I," but with the organism/environment field. The essential hostility of the ego to the physical organism and world is dissolved by a *reductio ad absurdum*, in which the most skillful means are employed to beguile the egocentric consciousness into consistent action upon its own premises. To what extent, then, are various forms of psychotherapy doing the same thing, however much their avowed objectives may have something else in mind?*

Haley's hypothesis can, I think, be used to show that many forms of psychotherapy with wide theoretical differences are using the same pattern of strategy as between the *guru* and his student. Yet it seems that, in many instances, the use of this strategy in psychotherapy is on a different level, perhaps less radical, and often with the object of fortifying the ego rather than of dissolving it. However, there are exceptions to this, and the confusion of terminology leaves some doubt as to the precise difference between a strong and responsible ego, on the one hand, and a unique and integrated individual, on the other.

Haley begins[140] with the assumption that psychopathological symptoms must be studied in the light of their function in any social context. How, in other words, do apparently involuntary symptoms of, say, anxiety, migraine, depression, alcoholism, phobia, or lethargy enable their victim to relate to other people? He suggests that such symptoms are strategic: they enable the person to control others without accepting responsibility for doing so, as when a mother prevents a daughter from marrying

---

* The problem is outside the scope of this book, but if there is a discrepancy between psychotherapeutic theories and the way in which they actually work, may there not be at least the potentiality of a similarly unconscious effectiveness in Christianity, such that it could become a way of liberation? Jesus's commandment, apparently addressed to the ego, "Thou *shalt* love the Lord thy God with all thy heart and with all thy soul and with all thy mind," is emphatically a double-bind. "You *must* be sincere." If taken as skillful means (*upaya*) rather than as a positive precept, these words could also be understood as a challenge to the ego and all its counsels of perfection. Jesus was certainly challenging the self-righteousness of the Pharisees, but we seem to have missed the humor of his equal challenge to Christians.

by becoming helplessly dependent on her undivided attention by some sort of invalidism. She is saying, in effect, that *she* is not requiring the daughter's attentions; her sickness requires them. The daughter cannot then refuse the bind without defining herself as inhumanly callous and undutiful, and she cannot accept it without denying her independence and her love for a man. Furthermore, the daughter cannot say, "But you are using this sickness to control me," without either insulting her mother or baffling her, for the mother simply cannot feel any responsibility for her symptoms. Thus the bind on the daughter is double. From Freud on it has seemed sound policy to look for the function or purpose of psychopathological symptoms, whether in the interpersonal context of social relations, or in the intrapersonal context of superego, ego, and id. The highly conjectural nature of the latter constellation gives greater probability to the former, in the sense of making it a more promising field of study.

Haley goes on to point out that in any social situation where one individual is putting double-binds upon others, the others respond with the same type of behavior. In the example cited, the mother wants the daughter's love — but the daughter cannot say, "I am staying home because I love you and because I want to." She has to say that she is acting involuntarily, because her mother is sick. In effect, the daughter is saying that she is loving her mother because she cannot help it, and does not want to — and now the mother is in a double-bind. She cannot get love from her daughter without realizing that it is not really love; and yet she cannot say, "Well, after all, you do not really love me," without the daughter's countering, "Then why do you think I am looking after you?" Furthermore, she cannot say, "You are just looking after me because you would feel ashamed to do otherwise"; she would not only be denying outright what she wants, love; she would also be giving away her own game. In this way, her symptoms are perpetuated. Because she has to be sick involuntarily, the daughter has to love her involuntarily, and therefore she has to be sick involuntarily. To get what they want, they are both doing what they don't want. They are in conflict and in misery, feeling themselves in the vicious circle of an insoluble problem.

It is worth pausing here to note a still deeper level of paradox. What do we mean when we ask to be loved voluntarily? We are *not* asking to be loved out of a sense of duty, which is what is ordinarily meant by a sense of responsibility. Willed, or forced, love — the ego trying to dominate emotion — is just what we don't want. Surely, what we are asking is that the other person love us because he cannot help it, that he love *in*voluntarily, but that the ego does not resist the emotion. We want the individual to enjoy his involuntary feeling for us. Confusion would be avoided by calling such love not voluntary, but spontaneous. Now the spontaneous is what happens of itself, the Taoist *tzu-jan* or "of itself so," what happens without forced effort. Spontaneity is not an ego action at all; on the contrary, it is action which the social control mechanism of the ego does not block. If anyone says, "With all my heart I love you," it is not the ego that speaks. He means that it is delightful to love spontaneously without blocking from and conflict with socially implanted notions of one's role, identity, and duty. When someone loves *first* out of a sense of duty, and later begins to like it, we may often suspect that what he has actually come to enjoy is the security of being obedient, of feeling again the warmth of parental approval.*

---

* In which case the object of love becomes a father or mother substitute and the relationship therefore implicitly incestuous; hence guilt and hence the genesis of a vicious circle.

Herein lies the profound confusion of so many of our ethical and marital conventions. Society may well be within its rights to require controls of the expression of spontaneity, to say, "On such occasions and in such ways you must *not* be spontaneous." But to say, "You *must* be spontaneous" is the flat contradiction at the root of every double-bind. Hypnosis alone can produce an apparently obedient spontaneity, and this is perhaps why "cures" based on simple hypnotherapy are so superficial and short-lived.

If, as Haley supposes, the task of the therapist is to break the double-binds imposed upon the patient and so stop him from imposing them on others, his basic objective must be to make the patient see the nonsense of demanding spontaneity. To this end he knowingly or unknowingly engages the patient in a therapeutic double-bind. It is therapeutic because the therapist does not really want to dominate the patient for his own ends, and because it is going to be directed in such a way as to reveal its own contradiction. In short, the patient becomes involved in a relationship which he cannot define or control however hard he may try.

From the very start the patient has to come as the suppliant. He has to define himself as in need of help; he has to pay for the privilege of consultation; he has to humiliate himself in saying that he cannot refrain from doing things that he does not want to do, that he is not in control of his own behavior. Every sound therapy resorts at this point to judo. The therapist does not deny the symptoms by saying, "Stop being nervous!" Nor does he deny the patient's feeling that he ought to be in control by saying, "Well, there's nothing you can do about it." Either response would end the relationship then and there. Instead, the therapist takes the side of the patient's ego against the symptoms; he accepts the patient's definition of the problem, and *allows* him, as perhaps other people do not, to be out of control. By having the therapist's permission to be sick, the patient is at once reassured and brought under the therapist's authority.

Let us suppose, now, that the therapist's method is one of the forms of psychoanalysis. He will then suggest that there are unconscious reasons for the difficulty. It matters little whether these be described as repressed traumas of infancy or concealed factors in interpersonal relationships. The point is to say either, "You are in difficulty because you do not understand yourself," or, "You do not really want to control your symptoms." In either case the competence of the ego is challenged, but at a new and higher level, for while the therapist has agreed that the ego is not in control he has questioned whether it "really" wants to be in control or whether it has defined the problem correctly. The patient may either accept or reject this suggestion, but if the latter, the therapist will not argue. He will simply ask, "I wonder why you seem so anxious to deny that possibility." He will imply, then, that the patient is resisting treatment, indirectly reinforcing the suggestion that he does not "really" want to get well. More indirectly still, he may suggest that the patient's desire to retain his symptoms is unconscious, or that the "unconscious" is producing them, acting as a sort of second self, more powerful than the ego.

The idea of the "unconscious" enables the patient to express and talk about himself without assuming responsibility for what he says. This pattern of communication is, of course, the same as using one's symptoms to control relationships. "It is happening, but I am not doing it and so cannot be blamed." By assuming an unconscious mind, the therapist accepts and encourages this behavior pattern, but at the same time he prevents the patient from using it to control *him*. On the one hand, the therapist takes authority for interpreting this indirect communication. Whether or not the therapist actually makes interpretations, the patient is given to understand that his dreams and free associations are intelligible to the therapist in a way that they are not intelligible to himself. On the other hand, the patient is apparently put in charge of the situation by being told to do the talking himself, to initiate the topics of discussion, and to bring up whatever "unconscious material" he pleases. But just because this is what the therapist has told him to do, his controlling the conversation is obedience to the therapist, and by this judo the patient is put in a double-bind. Try as he may to control the situation and to use communication from the "unconscious" to shield himself from unpleasant discoveries, he is always doing so at the therapist's direction. In other words, try as he may to shift responsibility to the therapist — "*You* tell me what to do; *you* cure me, tell me what is wrong with me, etc." — the fact is that this behavior is being commanded without being accommodated. In the transference, for example, the analyst becomes a parental figure upon whom the patient depends without being able to make him actually take responsibility. But a blunt refusal to take responsibility is never made, for this would no longer challenge the patient to try to control the therapist. He therefore avoids taking responsibility indirectly by saying, "I must help you to find out what *you* really want to do," or, "Let us wait and see what comes up from your own unconscious." In short, the therapist is directing the patient to try to control the relationship, but making it appear that he is not being directive at all and that everything is happening on the patient's own initiative.

However the patient tries to control the therapist, he is at once countered with a judo "ploy" which simultaneously frustrates the attempt and provokes a further effort. He is, furthermore, being allowed and encouraged to make the attempt in his characteristic way: unconsciously and irresponsibly, as by describing his dreams or free associations, which thus become extensions of his involuntary symptoms — an enlarged and enriched description of all behaviors which he does not claim as *his*. Naturally, he describes all this "unconscious material" in the hope that the therapist will tell him what it means, or that it will lead to a diagnosis for which the therapist can simply prescribe a remedy. But the therapist never refuses to do so directly. Instead he encourages more dreams and more free associations, as if these would elucidate what has gone before, or lead down into deeper and deeper regions of the unconscious. At the same time he is directing the patient to take charge of the situation by such questions as "Well, what do *you* think the dream means?"

In due course the double-bind on the patient becomes critical. He cannot get out of it by quitting the relationship, because the therapist has defined this as unconscious resistance to treatment or as admitting that he does not really want to get well. He cannot force the therapist to make decisions for him, because the relationship is always being defined by the therapist as supportive but nondirective. He cannot break out of the situation by aggression, by abusing the therapist, because the latter can never be fazed: he simply accepts the attack by going limp or by questioning its motivation, e.g., "I wonder if you don't like me because I remind you of someone else." According to Haley, at this critical point of frustration the patient has to give up, but he cannot give up by quitting. He can give up only by behaving in a different way; but what can he do?

Haley suggests that because the patient has in fact been offering his symptoms at the therapist's direction, he can escape from the therapeutic bind, from the therapist's control, only by losing interest in his symptoms and by ceasing to offer them. Alternatively, he can acknowledge that he has been trying unsuccessfully to control the therapist, and other people as well, by offering these symptoms — but in this case he has to claim them as his own behavior, to accept responsibility for them. The therapist's judo has provoked the patient to behave consistently in his symptomatic way, to the point of discovering that it is completely inappropriate and unsuccessful.

But I feel that something more needs to be said. Throughout all this the therapist has been testing two premises which the patient assumed from the outset. The first is that some of his actions are his own, and that they proceed freely from his ego. The second is that some of his actions are not his own, and that they happen spontaneously against his will. The therapist challenges the first premise by asking whether behavior which the patient believes to be voluntary is really so. "Do you really want to get well?" "I wonder what you really mean when you say that you don't like me." He challenges the second premise by attributing intent to involuntary behavior, suggesting that dreams express hidden wishes or questioning the significance of the patient's automatic gestures or nervous movements. This, too, is a double-bind because it implies that however the patient behaves, voluntarily or involuntarily, he reveals himself and that all his defenses are transparent to the therapist. Again, if he leaves the field, he is resisting. If he goes blank and tries to frustrate this maneuver by blocking himself, the therapist may gently imply that this, too, is revealing and that there must be something that he is extremely anxious to conceal from himself.

The other side of the fact that the patient is trying to control the therapist is that he is trying to get help without having to be aware of himself. What he actually is, is so inconsistent with his image of himself that he dare not find out, and yet he would not be coming for treatment at all unless he were dimly aware of the discrepancy. The therapist "bugs" the patient by suggesting that he cannot really conceal himself, but at the same time he indicates that his own attitude is one of complete acceptance and friendliness. Obviously, this situation is not established in a single consultation; it develops through the interaction of the two persons over a period of time. As the relationship proceeds, the patient discovers that all his attempts at blocking and self-concealment are absurd, that he is locked in a situation from which the only escape is simply to be what he is without restraint. The compliant patient may, of course, imitate spontaneity and positively gush with free associations, but the perceptive therapist detects and challenges every artifice until the patient can no longer be blocked or fazed.

At this point the patient simply stops pretending. He does not learn to "be himself" as if that were something which one can *do*; he learns rather that there is nothing he can do *not* to be himself. But this is just another way of saying that he has ceased to identify himself with his ego, with the image of himself which society has forced upon him. As a result of the therapist's challenge to the patient's two premises, his voluntary behavior and his involuntary behavior come together as one, and he finds out that his total behavior, his organism, is both and neither: it is spontaneous. One may call this integration of the "personality," actualization of the "self," or even the development of a new "ego structure"; but it does not correspond at all to the normal sense of ego or self as the directive agent behind action.

Whenever this is the outcome of therapy, it is, at least in principle, the same as liberation. It has integrated the individual with his own "external" world, that is, with his involuntary and spontaneous aspects. But it still does not fully challenge the presumed split between the organism as a whole and its environment. It does not, like the Eastern ways, challenge the conventions of perception, whereby sights and sounds are taken to be outside the organism, and whereby movements of the organism/environment boundary are taken to be initiated by the organism. One of the few approaches to something of this kind in the West is the relatively little-known school of Gestalt psychology. In *Gestalt Therapy*, by Perls, Hefferline, and Goodman, the authors state:

> It is meaningless to define a breather without air, a walker without gravity and ground, an irascible without obstacles, and so on for every animal function. The definition of an organism is the definition of an organism/environment field; and the contact-boundary is, so to speak, the specific organ of awareness of the novel situation in the field....In the case of a stationary plant...the osmotic membrane is the *organ of the interaction* of organism and environment, both parts being obviously active. In the case of a mobile complicated animal it is the same, but certain illusions of perception make it more difficult to conceive. The illusions, to repeat them, are simply that the mobile wins attention against the stationary background, and the more tightly complicated wins attention against the relatively simpler. But at the boundary, the interaction is proceeding from both parts.[41]

One might prefer Bentley's "transaction" to "interaction," but otherwise this is a perfect description of the illusion-creating factor of the Buddhist *avidya* — "ignore-ance." The theoretical work of these authors is magnificent, but when it comes to therapy itself the technique rests too much upon trying deliberately to feel relationship. Experimental challenging of the illusions of separateness is far more convincing, because the final experience of the organism/environment field is a revelation and not an artificial construction. In general, however, it is the one-sidedly psychological emphasis of Western therapies which obstructs this further extension of liberation.

If, then, the essential technique of therapy is to challenge the patient's false and neurotic assumptions so that the more he holds to them, the more he finds himself in a double-bind, it seems to make little difference whether the theory be Freudian, Jungian, Rogerian, Existential, Interpersonal, or simply eclectic. The extreme nondirective theory of Carl Rogers is just as much a judo imposing double-binds as the more directive theory of, say, John Rosen.[142] Once two people enter into a relationship it is simply impossible for one of them, the therapist, to be so passive that he serves as nothing more than a mirror to the patient. As Haley points out, just to accept what the patient says or does is already to permit his behavior and thus take control of it.

> Whatever a therapist says or does not say in response to a patient will circumscribe the patient's behavior. Even if a therapist says, "I'm not going to tell you what to do," when a patient asks for direction, he is still directing the patient not to ask him what to do. If a patient complains to a therapist and the therapist is silent, this silence is inevitably a comment on the patient's behavior.[143]

What, then, is more of a double-bind than a situation in which the therapist is directing the patient by being completely nondirective? Rosen's directive judo is simply a different application of the same principle. For example, by commanding the patient to produce his symptoms, or even to exaggerate them, he takes control of what the patient does even if the patient does not produce them — for the context of the situation is therapeutic and thus the therapist's aim is to get rid of the symptoms. He wins either way!

All this may seem to be a tremendous oversimplification of therapy, but it is of the utmost importance to understand that the principle cannot be *used* in the simplified form in which it has been *described*. For one thing, the patient would see through it too easily and refuse the challenge. For another, applying it as a counter to the specific maneuvers of particular patients requires great versatility, practice, and judgment of character — though more in the way that a novelist or shrewd salesman judges character than a theoretical psychologist. We saw that the ways of liberation make much use of *upaya*, of skillful or "tricky" means, to challenge their students. The description of dreams, the production of fantasies and free associations, and the discussion of their symbolism constitute, I believe, *upaya*. It is necessary and therapeutic hocus-pocus, but it would be of very great help to the therapist to realize it. The difficulty of such theoretical systems as the Freudian and Jungian is that patients come away from therapy believing in them as religions. "Getting religion" may sometimes be effective therapy, if not liberation, but when the attention of therapists is set exclusively upon, say, dream symbolism, they lose sight not only of the essential technique of therapy but also of the social context of psychopathology.

This is not, of course, to say that the Freudian and Jungian theoretical systems are *pure* hocus-pocus without the least scientific value. Naturally, hypotheses which have had scientific value in the past may have less today, but the point is that to a very great extent these theories *function* as hocus-pocus in therapy. We saw, for instance, that telling a patient that he has an "unconscious mind" enables him to communicate with the therapist indirectly, without having to feel that *he* is responsible for what he says: it is the unconscious. This may not be acceptable to hard-core Freudians and Jungians, but if such individuals are to represent themselves in any sense as scientists nothing could be more inappropriate than a rigid theoretical party line. It is a great disadvantage to any therapist to have an ax to grind, because this gives him a personal interest in winning the countergame with his patient. But we saw, in reference to the Zen master, that he can play the game effectively just because winning or losing makes no difference to him. In the absence of this essential qualification, psychotherapy degenerates into a power game in which the therapist double-binds unfortunate patients for years and years for nothing but his own satisfaction.

This whole view of psychotherapy retains certain elements of these classical theories. It still seems quite proper to describe the ego as a construct of the reality principle (social convention) exercising repression upon life processes which thereby become more or less unconscious. It still seems valid to suppose that in the formation of the ego feeling the effects of training in infancy and childhood are of immense importance, even if it may not be necessary to recall them in therapy. As a result, it is surely true that the child's attitudes toward father and mother influence his attitudes to other people in later life, making him give and receive demands for forced spontaneity. It still seems to be true that, for Western cultures at least, the repression of sexuality is a major source of psychopathological behavior. Furthermore, Jung's constant insistence upon therapy as a reconciliation of opposites and upon the acceptance and assimilation of the Shadow, the dark and repressed aspect of one's nature, is quite central to this view of liberation. The problem is always that acceptance of oneself can never be a deliberate act; it is as paradoxical as kissing one's own lips. But the countergame challenges the actual possibility of rejecting oneself, and in the end it does not construct but *reveals* the wholeness of man as an inescapable fact.

From this point of view we can also see a new significance in Freud's attribution of a sexual character to unconscious motivation — that is, if we take it as therapeutic strategy rather than psychological fact. In any culture which is sexually squeamish, the suggestion that one's real motivations are sexual is a peculiarly effective challenge to the ego. Just because the culture regards sexuality as evil or degrading, the suggestion implies that one's true motivations are the *opposite* of one's conscious intention and thus that the ego is not really in charge of things at all. When the individual is strongly identified with his ego, such a suggestion is at once resisted, and then the therapist has only to point out that the patient would have no reason to deny the suggestion so energetically if it were not true. He is thereby put in the position of denying his ego by the very act of affirming it, and the double-bind thus imposed is all the more effective because he cannot honestly deny the existence of sexual feeling and its inevitable attraction. If the therapist's intention were to attack and accuse the patient, we might feel that this strategy gave him a very unfair advantage. But in fact the imposition of this particular bind simply exposes the bind which has already been imposed upon the patient by society. He would never have fallen into the therapist's "trap" if he had not first been tricked into disowning himself and his own feelings by accepting the fiction that *he* is his ego or soul, and not his entire organism.

To escape from the therapist's trap, the patient can only stop defending himself against himself, and in dropping this defense he ceases, at the same time, to identify himself with the ego.

But this can happen only as it becomes clear to the patient that the therapist is not attacking him, which in turn depends upon the therapist's having genuinely accepted himself. This means, however, that the therapist represents a philosophy other than that of society and stands, as it were, for the authority of nature rather than for the authority of men. But this becomes the superior authority only as it can be shown that social authority contains a self-contradiction from which natural authority is free, and a self-contradiction so basic that its perpetuation must destroy society and drive men to madness.

VI. Invitation to the Dance

The saying "By their fruits ye shall know them" is generally taken to mean that men are finally to be judged by their moral behavior, and philosophies of life by their moral consequences. But the only definition of morality which can today command any general assent is: conduct which furthers the survival of society. We understand the fruits of thought and action as their nutritive utility; that fruits may be lovely in taste and texture is quite incidental. The question is only whether they contain the proper vitamins, and taste is important only insofar as it facilitates digestibility. In such a morality the function of play is to make work tolerable, and work is a burden, not because it requires more effort than play, but because it is a contest with death. Work as we know it is contaminated with the fear of death, for work is what *must* be done in order to survive, and to survive, to go on, is the ultimate and irreducible necessity. Why is it not obvious that to make survival necessary is to make it a burden? Life is above all a spontaneous process, and, as we have seen, to command spontaneity, to say that one *must* live, is the basic contradiction imposing the double-bind on us all.

To take sides is always the first step in a *game*, and to choose life as against death, being as against nonbeing, is only to pretend that they are separable. Yet it is represented to us as the ultimately serious choice. The prototypes of being and nonbeing are doubtless matter and space, form and emptiness, and it was perhaps inevitable that we should have thought of matter as enjoying a precarious and transitory existence in the midst of infinite and eternal nothingness. But it seems almost certain that modern astronomy and cosmology are coming close to a vision of the universe where space is no longer the inert container of the galaxies but an integral part of their form. Form encloses space just as much as space encloses form. Speaking metaphorically, it is as if space and form lay together upon the surface of a sphere in such a way that the choice as to which is figure and which background is quite arbitrary. Life, or formative process, is not therefore happening within some alien continuum that is not life.

In the sleep of "ignore-ance," of narrowed attention which does not see things whole, our gaze is captured by the convenient figure rather than by its ground, or counterfigure. But the awakening of liberation is to realize that all choices between "opposites" are the separation of inseparables. In the words of the Zen master Seng-ts'an:

> The perfect Way [Tao] is without difficulty,
> Save that it avoids picking and choosing....
> If you want to get the plain truth,
> Be not concerned with right and wrong.
> The conflict between right and wrong
> Is the sickness of the mind.[144]

The point is not that one stops choosing, but that one chooses in the knowledge that there is really no choice. Eastern philosophy is full of such seeming paradoxes — to act without action, to think without thought, to love without attachment. It is simply that in a universe of relativity, all choosing, all taking of sides, is playful. But this is not that one feels no urgency. To know the relativity of light and darkness is not to be able to gaze unblinkingly into the sun; to know the relativity of up and down is not to be able to fall upward. To feel urgency without compulsion is the seemingly paradoxical way of describing what it is like for a feeling to arise spontaneously without its happening to a feeler.

What, then, are the fruits of liberation if it sets one free from the morality of survival and flight from death? It is only natural that we should be disturbed at the thought that people live among us who do not take the social game seriously. How will they behave if they do not ultimately believe in our rules? The question applies also to psychotherapy, and it has been asked again and again ever since Freud connected neurosis with repression. Freud and the psychoanalysts have not really faced the question because they have never seriously considered doing away with repression. On the whole, they have taken the side of the reality principle, of the superego and the ego against the id. But at the same time they have softened the conflict, and the social effect of Freud's doctrine has been tremendous, not only in bringing about a greater degree of sexual freedom but also in changing our ideas of individual responsibility. The whole recognition that deviants, delinquents, and criminals are sick rather than sinful and need psychotherapy rather than punishment stems directly from Freud, and has become characteristic of all liberal and "progressive" social reform. Nevertheless, there are many who fear that the Freudian ethic is seriously undermining

our society, for as a result of it there are more and more people who do not accept full responsibility for their actions. The
blame for one's behavior can be shifted indefinitely, and without
a good old-fashioned sense of guilt we seem to lose not only an
effective deterrent to evil but also a sense of human dignity.

Freud, it must be remembered, remained a dualist in his
view of human nature, and so long as there seems to be a basic
incompatibility between instinct and reason, Eros and civilization, there must remain an insoluble moral problem — to which
repression only *seems* to be a workable answer. Thus, in defining
the problem of education Freud said:

> The child has to learn to control its instincts. To grant it
> complete freedom, so that it obeys all its impulses without
> any restriction, is impossible. It would be a very instruc-
> tive experiment for child-psychologists, but it would make
> life impossible for the parents and would do serious dam-
> age to the children themselves.... Education has therefore
> to steer its way between the Scylla of giving the instincts
> free play and the Charybdis of frustrating them.[145]

It may be necessary to divide the child against itself for the purpose of learning certain patterns of social behavior, but if the
child does not later in life discover that this division was, like the
myth of Santa Claus, a trick, it turns into a permanently alienated
personality. When such personalities, in their turn, bring up children they impose the division upon them without knowing that
it is a trick, and thus their admonitions are given without humor
and often without essential kindness. For when the child is recal-
citrant, the self-alienated adult is genuinely furious; he does not
realize that bringing up children is playing a game with them.

The practical problem of repression as a human disease does
not, therefore, require that we stop disciplining our children. It

is more simply a question of realizing that when we teach them to think of themselves as the duality of ego and instinct, controller and controlled, this is nothing but strategy. The practical problem is for adults, and it is the problem which Norman Brown has stated so masterfully in his *Life against Death*: Is it not time that we carried Freud's thought to its full conclusion and learned to live without repression? The question is at first sight outrageous, which is just what makes Brown's sophisticated and scholarly book all the more impressive. Yet if the question could be answered affirmatively, the fruits of liberation would really be fruits. The results which the practical moralist demands from any change in consciousness, from the mystical vision, are not really fruits at all. He wants self-sacrifice, courage, and dedication as a means to the continuation of social life. But there is absolutely no point in clothing the naked, feeding the hungry, and healing the sick if it is just that they may live to be naked, hungry, and sick again, or live merely to be able to do the same for others. Practical morality, whether Judaic or Christian, capitalist or communist, is provision for a future — a perpetual renunciation or postponement. This is a future which no one is ever going to be able to enjoy because, by the time it arrives, everyone will have lost the ability to live in the present. Thus the test of liberation is not whether it issues in good works; the test of good works is whether they issue in liberation — in the capacity to *be* all that one is without repression or alienation. On the principle that "the Sabbath is made for man, and not man for the Sabbath," the function of moral behavior is always secondary and subordinate.

But to what? One has the impression that the ways of liberation, like Catholic Christianity, conceive the *summum bonum*, the true end of man, to be eternal contemplation and enjoyment of the bodiless and spiritual Godhead in a future life beyond death.

Yet when the Eastern ways are understood more deeply, it appears that *Nirvana* is not after, beyond, or away from birth-and-death (*samsara*), but that, in the Zen master Hakuin's words:

> *This very earth is the Lotus Land of purity,*
> *And this very body the Body of Buddha.*[146]

Eternity is now, and in the light of unrepressed vision the physical organism and the physical world turn out to be the divine world. But so long as life is work-against-death this cannot be seen. As Brown says:

> This incapacity to die, ironically but inevitably, throws mankind out of the actuality of living, which for all normal animals is at the same time dying; the result is denial of life (repression).... The distraction of human life to the war against death, by the same inevitable irony, results in death's dominion over life. The war against death takes the form of a preoccupation with the past and the future, and the present tense, the tense of life, is lost.[147]

Thereupon the business of life is guided by the neurotic repetition compulsion, the quest for survival, for more and more time in which we hope by some miracle to grasp what always eludes us in the present. It is thus that, starting from Freud, Brown can come to the same conclusion as Hakuin:

> If we connect — as Freud did not — the repetition-compulsion with Freud's reiterated theorem that the instinctual processes of the id are timeless, then only repressed life is in time, and unrepressed life would be timeless or in eternity. Thus again psychoanalysis, carried to its logical conclusion and transformed into a theory of history, gathers to itself ageless religious aspirations. The Sabbath of Eternity, that time when time no more shall be,

is an image of that state which is the ultimate goal of the repetition-compulsion in the timeless id....Psychoanalysis comes to remind us that we are bodies, that repression is of the body, and that perfection would be the realm of Absolute Body; eternity is the mode of unrepressed bodies.[148]

The final aim of psychoanalysis must therefore be a veritable resurrection of the body as distinct from some future reanimation of the corpse.

The aim of psychoanalysis — still unfulfilled, and still only half-conscious — is to return our souls to our bodies, to return ourselves to ourselves, and thus to overcome the human state of self-alienation....What orthodox psychoanalysis has in fact done is to reintroduce the soul-body dualism in its own new lingo, by hypostatizing the "ego" into a substantial essence which by means of "defense mechanisms" continues to do battle against the "id." Sublimation is disposed of by listing it as a "successful" defense mechanism. In substantializing the ego, orthodox psychoanalysis follows the authority of Freud, who compared the relation of the ego to the id to that of a rider to his horse — a metaphor going back to Plato's *Phaedrus* and perpetuating the Platonic dualism.[149]

Orthodox psychoanalysis has thus allied itself with the reality principle and the ethics of survival. Its issue is not "a union with others and with the world around us based not on anxiety and aggression but on narcissism and erotic exuberance";[150] it is the dull thud, the anemic anticlimax of what Philip Rieff has called "psychological man."

The psychological ideal of normality has a rather unheroic aspect. Think of a whole society dominated by psychotherapeutic ideals. Considered not from the individual's but from a sociological point of view, psychoanalysis is an expression of a popular tyranny such as not even de Tocqueville adequately imagined.... In the emergent democracy of the sick, everyone can to some extent play doctor to others, and none is allowed the temerity to claim that he can definitively cure or be cured. The hospital is succeeding the church and the parliament as the archetypal institution of Western culture.[51]

For this is the tame and insipid consequence of a middle way in which the opposites are not transcended but compromised, where there is no more than a cautious treaty between the rider and the horse, the soul and the body, the ego and the id.

As we have seen, the failure of orthodox psychoanalysis is the result of Freud's dualism, and thus of the fear that the unrepressed human body will turn out to be a wild animal rutting and snarling in the squalor of its own excrement. Biologically and morphologically man may be an animal, but he is *not* a horse, a tiger, or a baboon. The unique structure of his organism and brain enables him to discipline himself, but it is simply pretense that this self-control is based upon an actual dualism of soul and body, ego and id. The pretense may be useful as a temporary measure, as a pedagogical gambit; but when it becomes the permanent cast of human feeling, it is nothing more than an artificial prolongation of childhood tutelage, a failure to grow up which makes all the disciplines of culture abortive. For when the pretense remains unconscious and is taken to be real, the soul thus abstracted from the body is abstracted from the organ of enjoyment. It becomes chronically afraid to be physical and to participate completely in physical spontaneity. As a result, the man identified with the soul is always frustrated and always needs more time. Because he knows that the body will die, its corruptible form becomes his enemy. The disciplines of art and science are therefore pressed into service in the war against death, against the body, and against spontaneity. Morality, too, becomes the servant of the discarnate soul.

But everything that fights against the body and death becomes death, that is, becomes incapable of spontaneity and therefore of genuine delight. The quest for future satisfaction is consequently a vicious circle, and cultural progress becomes the course of its ever more frantic attempts to solve the self-contradictory problem. It is no answer to abandon the disciplines of art, science, and morality in the current style of "beat-ism." The real problem is to put these disciplines at the disposal of spontaneity. For when we have Eros dominated by reason instead of Eros expressing itself with reason, we create a culture that is simply against life, in which the human organism has to submit more and more to the needs of mechanical organization, to postpone enjoyment in the name of an ever more futile utility.

When cultural disciplines are in the service of Eros, ethics are transformed from the rules of repression into the technique of expression, and morality becomes the aesthetics of behavior.

> The discipline of aesthetics installs the *order of sensuousness* as against the *order of reason*. Introduced into the philosophy of culture, this notion aims at a liberation of the senses which, far from destroying civilization, would give it a firmer basis and would greatly enhance its potentialities. Operating through a basic impulse — namely, the play impulse — the aesthetic function would "abolish compulsion, and place man, both morally and physically, in freedom." It would harmonize the feelings and affections with the ideas of reason, deprive the "laws of reason

of their moral compulsion," and "reconcile them with the interest of the senses."[152]

Marcuse, here quoting Schiller, seems to be reviving the "discredited" idealism of the eighteenth-century romantics, the naturalistic optimism which the two world wars are supposed to have demonstrated to be a false philosophy. But in no sense are the wars and revolutions of modern times examples of what happens when civilized repression is removed. They are the outbursts of sadistic rage for which the civilization of repression must always provide; they are its price, but a technological civilization can no longer afford the price. But for the same reason — as Marcuse argues — it does not need to pay it. For the technology which makes these outbursts insanely destructive also makes the culture of repression unnecessary because, in principle, it abolishes the need for drudgery and labor. Yet technology is not permitted to abolish labor because

> ...of all things, hard work has become a virtue instead of the curse which it was always advertised to be by our remote ancestors.... Our children should be prepared to bring their children up so they won't have to work as a neurotic necessity. The necessity to work is a neurotic symptom. It is a crutch. It is an attempt to make oneself feel valuable even though there is no particular need for one's working.[153]

When technology is used — quite absurdly — to increase employment rather than to get rid of it, work becomes "busywork" — an artificial creation of ever more meaningless routines, an interminable production of things that are not so much luxuries for physical gratification as pretentious trash. Technology then works against Eros and, as a result, labor is all the more alienated and the necessity for violent outbursts increased. As Marcuse says, "to link performances on assembly lines, in offices and shops with instinctual needs is to glorify dehumanization as pleasure."[154] The type of human being who submits to this culture is, almost literally, a zombie. He is docile and "mature" in the style of our drab and dismal bourgeoisie; he is quite incapable of gaiety or exuberance; he believes that he is dancing when he is shuffling around a room; he thinks he is being entertained when he is passively watching a couple of muscle-bound thugs in a wrestling match; he thinks he is being scholarly and intellectual when he is learning to speak with modesty and "all due reservations" about some minor Elizabethan playwright; worse still, he thinks he is rebelling against all this when he grows a beard and gets himself a dingy "pad" in the slums. This is the *only* major movement of dissent, apart from the protest against racial segregation, now current in the United States!

This is not, of course, a balanced and considered opinion; it is an expression of feeling, but not without very evident grounds. The tragedy is that both the ways of liberation in the East and psychotherapy in the West have, to so large an extent, been sidetracked into the war against death and therefore into alienation from the body and from spontaneity. While the swami and the monk are poisoned with addiction to their own medicine and, out of false humility, simply do not dare to be liberated, the "psychological man" — be he therapist or graduate patient — walks with solemn balance along his tightrope between too much Logos and too much Eros. As Rieff says:

> Being essentially negative, normality is an ever-retreating ideal. An attitude of stoic calm is required for its pursuit. No one catches the normal; everyone must act as if it can be caught. Nor can the psychological man forget himself

in pursuit of the normal, for his normality consists of a certain kind of self-awareness.[155]

As the run-of-the-mill yogi is permanently *on the way* to liberation, so there is a tendency for the analyst and the analysand alike to be permanently "bugged," to be always suspicious of themselves, and thus to avoid any behavior — outside the consulting room — which might be taken to be unconscious. The absence of spontaneity at almost any gathering of psychotherapists is one of the sorriest sights in the world.

The question as to what a society of liberated people would be like is perhaps academic. What would happen if everyone in Manhattan decided to catch the same train for New Haven? Yet as the ideas of Freud, however twisted, have had the most far-reaching social influence, it is not impossible that ideas derived from the ways of liberation and from such revolutionary interpreters of psychoanalysis as Norman Brown may stir up something far more disturbing and energetic and exuberant than the Beat Generation. Some of their popular perversions are going to be devastating, but, even so, far preferable to anything foreshadowed in Huxley's *Brave New World*, Orwell's *1984*, and even to much of the dreary sobriety that already surrounds us. It is still far from certain, as Richard LaPiere[156] and others contend, that the Freudian ethic itself has actually increased social irresponsibility, for there was never a moralist at any time who was not certain that things were going from bad to worse.

Delinquency has been with us from the time man began trying to civilize himself by establishing certain social codes of behavior. John Locke, the great English educator, three hundred years ago deplored delinquency in the same vein as we do today. Six thousand years ago an

Egyptian priest carved on a stone, "Our earth is degenerate.... Children no longer obey their parents."[157]

LaPiere's case for the "subversion of American character," of
the enterprising Protestant ethic, by the Freudian view of human
nature simply recoils upon itself. In urging the ever-growing
need for men of idealism and enterprise to cope with the problems which technological civilization is piling up for us, it is by
no means beside the point to note that men of idealism and enterprise, busily at war with death, created the problem in the
first place. Certainly, the problem cannot be abandoned, but it
would be insane to go on wrestling with it in the same spirit that
created it — the spirit of alienation from nature and ecological
blindness.

If the Freudian ethic is demoralizing, it is not because it has
revealed the unconscious springs of action beyond control of the
ego. It is because it has retained the ego as the subjective experiment and puppet of the instincts and of social conditioning alike,
and this has, if anything, increased the isolation of man-as-ego
from his organic life on the one hand and from his fellow men
on the other. For an impotent ego is more alienated than one
which feels itself fully in control. The position of psychoanalysis
is paradoxical because it is a step in the right direction which has
not gone nearly far enough. It is attacked for the poverty of its
results, and yet it has uncovered so many facts which can hardly
be denied.

But the ethical problem is completely relevant if it is put in
its proper place. Liberation is not the release of the soul from the
body; it is recovery from the tactical split between the soul and
the body which seems to be necessary for the social discipline of
the young. It therefore sets reason and culture not against Eros
but at the disposal of Eros, of the "polymorphous perverse"

body which always retains the potentiality of a fully erotic relationship with the world — not just through the genital system but through the whole sensory capacity. Liberation restores the "primary narcissism" not just of the organism by itself, but of the organism/environment field. It is thus quite pertinent to ask how this "narcissism" might express itself ethically, or what, in other words, might be the ethics of Eros and of spontaneity as distinct from the ethics of survival.

It simplifies things to think of ethical behavior as a language, for like language proper, like art and music, it is a form of communication. But among all moralists, religious and otherwise, there is a tendency to treat ethics as a dead language, and to use it as Latin is used in the Catholic Church. In other words, authority shows a far greater resistance to ethical innovation and change than to comparable changes in language and the arts. Yet, in spite of this, the forms of ethical expression do in fact change, but the official versions tend to recognize these changes only by rather reluctant reinterpretation of such ancient standards and formulations as the Ten Commandments. There is obviously no guarantee that the ethics of Eros would be expressed in any such "Bronze-Age" terms.

It has almost always been man's custom to look for the authority for ethical standards outside ethics, to the laws of nature or the laws of God. We have never felt fully free to base our ethical principles simply upon what we would like to do and to have done to us, for fear that such experimental conduct might injure us in unforeseen ways. There is obvious sense, up to a point, in sticking to what has worked in the past (if, indeed, it has), but equally obvious nonsense in attributing past formulations to a wisdom greater than ours. It is all very well to believe that "Mother is always right" until you yourself are a mother, but the constant attribution of a mysterious wisdom to antiquity is all bound up with our failure to recover from being children. We forget that we are being unnecessarily impressed by ancestors, who also failed to recover from childhood and who, for that reason, revered authorities in the same predicament as themselves.

Nevertheless, tradition in ethics has the same sort of importance as tradition in language: it is simply the way in which people get to know what the rules are. One must therefore respect ethical tradition in the same way that one must respect linguistic or artistic tradition: not because it is sacrosanct, but because it is the only way of being in communication with others. If I wish to make an innovation in language acceptable, I must point out its meaning in the terms and the context of language as it already exists, for a completely abrupt change will not be understood. In Western culture, for example, the rules of painting and music have changed far more rapidly than the rules of speech, so that time after time the public has been shocked by paintings and compositions which seem incomprehensible. The early Beethoven symphonies provoked as much dismay at first hearing as the work of any of the great moderns, and the first reaction to such communications is not generally that they are difficult but that they are *bad*. The public feels that the artist has lost control of his technique. But later, if we try to understand what he is doing, we find that he has greatly enriched our experience. The artist's problem is to avoid changing the rules so radically that no bridge remains over which the public can follow him.

Now there are always purists and conservatives who will insist that there are absolute standards of correct speech and aesthetic technique. They will maintain, for example, that the ear has a fixed structure to which only one set of musical rules is appropriate, and anyone who claims to enjoy music composed by other rules will be accused of having perverse ears or of deceiving himself. There are even those who would like to freeze the English language into the form in which it was spoken, say, in upper-class London in 1900 — though why not 1800 or even 1600? One will not deny that dead languages, like Sanskrit and Church Latin, have certain technical uses, but spoken languages in daily usage change whether one likes it or not. The task of the grammarian and lexicographer is to maintain orderly change — not to lay down the law, but to stabilize linguistic change by keeping all members of a society informed as to what rules are being used.

Our culture inherits from both Jerusalem and Rome an ethical philosophy analogous to code law rather than common law. For wherever we ask what we *ought* to do, and seek authority for ethical standards either in the will of God or in the laws of nature, we assume a preexisting pattern, like a legal code or like roads and rails, to which human behavior is supposed to conform. This is much more than asking only that human behavior proceed in a pattern that is consistent with its own past — that it refrain from unintelligible jumps. Common law, on the other hand, makes itself up as it goes along; it sets precedents but they are never unalterable, because they are derived ultimately not from a book of rules, but from a judge's intuitive feeling for equity and fair play — from a man rather than a machine. Code law assumes a pattern laid down once and for all; common law assumes a freely developing pattern which is nevertheless consistent with itself, like the development of a living language.

Now if liberation brings about the subordination of reason to Eros, as distinct from the subordination of Eros to reason, it is obviously allied to common law rather than code law. The ultimate authority for behavior does not, then, lie in any verbal formulation of oughts and ought-nots; it lies in the order of the organism/environment, an order which can never be fully or finally formulated in any stated laws of nature. Expecting scientific description to discover the pattern to which nature conforms is really assuming that law, or verbal formulation, precedes physical behavior — following the ancient notion that God *told* the universe what to do. But if we see that nature, instead of *conforming to* a pattern, *is* a pattern, we can get rid of a redundant and confusing step in our thinking. To say that reason is subordinate to Eros is simply to say that it is feedback, that it serves Eros by feeding back a description of spontaneous action. In just the same way, scientific description follows the pattern of nature; it does not lay down, like rails, the rules which nature *must* follow, for the pattern itself is developing freely. The feedback, the description, simply helps the human pattern to develop in a more orderly fashion. What reason and science are thus serving, and what always remains, therefore, the authority for action, is the body, and the order of the body is not mechanical but organic.*

We saw that common law rests ultimately upon the judge's intuitive feeling for equity. Every case is unique, and no code or set of fixed principles can provide for every eventuality. The deciding factor is therefore something far more subtle and complex than any formulation of rules can be — the judge's brain, *assisted* by precedents and rules. Code law, as well as authoritarian and traditionalist ethics, subverts the hierarchy of nature. It gives greater trust and authority to the relatively crude and

---

* For a fuller discussion of the difference between mechanical and organic order see Watts,[18] and also the brilliant discussion by Needham[19] of the relation of Chinese ideas of natural order to Chinese law.

rigid structure of verbal rules than to the infinitely more fluid and complex structure of the brain, the organism, and the field in which they live. Liberation returns us to the natural hierarchy, and I say "hierarchy" because it is a pattern in which reason and verbal rules are subordinated but not obliterated.

There are, then, two main reasons for comparing ethics with language and art. The first is to stress their aesthetic character, to say that they must work as a technique for expressing Eros or what Marcuse calls "the order of sensuousness," and thus put them in their proper place in the hierarchy. Ethics are then subordinate to spontaneity as in Lao-tzu's description of the ascending levels of natural order:

> The model [or law] of man is the earth;
> The model of the earth is heaven;
> The model of heaven is the Tao;
> The model of the Tao is spontaneity.[160]

From this follows the second reason: to show that the function of ethics is not directive, but advisory and suggestive. Their creative use can no more be prescribed than we can write down simple instructions for making masterpieces of poetry or painting. But just as the inspired use of language is impossible without knowledge of the language, there can be no ethical expression of Eros to a repressed society without tact, that is, without a familiarity with the conventions of the society, with the channels open to communication and the blocks in its way.

For the joyous task which confronts an ethic of spontaneity, however difficult it may be, is quite literally to woo people out of their armed shells. But where in either East or West has this been seriously proposed? The forces working for social change never seem to think of summoning Eros to their aid. The tyranny of civilized masochism (of which the exploiters themselves are victims) cannot, as communism supposes, be overthrown by armed revolution. What is gained by force must be held by force, and for this reason the communist culture is, if anything, still more against life than the capitalist, and still more committed to the ethics of survival. On the other hand, the social idealism of Gandhi or of the Quakers is *also* a way of violence, of spiritual violence against the body, making its appeal to the masochism of "self-sacrifice." Admirable, devoted, and sincere as its followers are, the love which they are expressing is a blend of duty and pity, a soul love in which there is no erotic warmth or gaiety, and which therefore fails to express the whole man. The idealisms which civilization produces are strivings of the alienated soul against death, and because their appeal is to hostility, to fear, to pity (which is also fear), or to duty, they can never arouse the energy of life itself — Eros — which alone has the power to put reason into practice.

If there is anything to be learned from history, it is that scoldings, warnings, and preachings are a complete ethical failure. They may serve as part of the mummery with which children are hurried into learning adult conventions, but as the general means of inducing social change they only confirm and ingrain the attitudes which keep us at war. Psychoanalysis in the West and the ways of liberation in the East should enable us to see that the only effective way is to appeal to Eros, without which Logos — the sense of duty and reason — has no life. The problem is that civilized man has learned to be so deeply afraid of Eros that he scorns any suggestion that social love must be erotic; it conjures images of something slimy, lustful, fawning, and obscene which he wants to crush like a loathsome insect. As we have seen, this is in part because the erotic as he knows it is restricted to the genital and does not irradiate the whole sensory field, and thus he imagines that erotic fellowship with others would be a collective sexual orgy. At a deeper level, the fear of the erotic is the dissociated soul's resentment of its mortal body — failing to see that death is a problem not for the organism, but for the soul. It is thus that so much of the organism's spontaneous behavior is shameful: it denies the ego's claim to be master.

But to appeal to Eros, psychoanalysis must overcome the remnants of antagonism in its own attitude to culture, and its use of a jargon which still carries the implication that the erotic is disgusting. So often the psychoanalytic interpretation of culture seems to be nothing more than debunking. It finds erotic symbolism in all the deliberate creations of art, science, and religion as if to say, "What dirty animals you are after all!" But Freud's detection of the erotic in everything supposedly spiritual and sublime is really a marvelous revelation. It shows that, try as we may, spontaneity cannot be prevented, and the fact that man is a living organism cannot be concealed. There is no reason for shame in the recognition that our most lofty images and conceptions have an erotic symbolism. Psychotherapy and liberation are completed in the moment when shame and guilt collapse, when the organism is no longer compelled to defend itself for being an organism, and when the individual is ready to own his unconscious behavior. But psychoanalysis does not, in practice, make it clear that the erotic is deeper than the genital. Beyond the play of the penis in the vagina lies the play of the organism in its environment — the polymorphous eroticism of man's original body as it comes from the womb.

"Polymorphous eroticism" is by no means a fancy term for hedonism, for the mere pursuit of pleasure on all fronts. As Coomaraswamy said, spontaneity (*sahaja*) is "a path of non-pursuit," whereas the *pursuit* of pleasure implies an organism's assaulting its environment to "get something out of it," as if the environment were not part and parcel of the organism. Like the complete sexual orgasm, the delight of this eroticism must "come" unforced. There is no self-conscious exercise in deliberately relaxing or opening the senses that can bring it about, save as an *upaya*, a technique to show that it cannot be commanded. Polymorphous eroticism can neither be cultivated nor made into a cult; it can only develop of itself when the soul has been returned to the body and the individual is no longer identified with the ego. It is thus that the adult recovers what in Zen is called the "natural endowment" which he had as a child, and this is why the Taoists see in the body of the child a model for the body of the sage. In the words of Chuang-tzu:

> Can you be like a newborn child? The baby cries all day and yet his voice never becomes hoarse; that is because he has not lost nature's harmony.... The baby looks at things all day without winking; that is because his eyes are not focussed on any particular object. He goes without knowing where he is going, and stops without knowing what he is doing. He merges himself with the surroundings and moves along with it. These are the principles of mental hygiene.[161]

This is Freud's "primal narcissism," and as Norman Brown says:

> Freud says not only that the human ego-feeling once embraced the whole world, but also that Eros drives the ego to recover that feeling: "The development of the ego consists in a departure from primal narcissism and results in a vigorous attempt to recover it." In primal narcissism the self is at one with a world of love and pleasure; hence the ultimate aim of the human ego is to reinstate what Freud calls "limitless narcissism" and find itself once more at one with the whole world in love and pleasure.[162]

The adult or mature version of primal narcissism is, of course, "cosmic consciousness," or the shift from egocentric awareness to the feeling that one's identity is the whole field of the organism in its environment. But if this is not to remain a purely contemplative state, if, in other words, the liberated man is to return into the world like the bodhisattva, he will seek the means for expressing his sense of being "at one with the whole world in love and pleasure." Because the means are aesthetic his approach to the world is, as Marcuse suggests, that of Orpheus, "the priest, the mouthpiece of the gods," who tames both men and beasts by the allure and magic of his harp. His method is not that of the preacher or the politician but that, in its widest sense, of the artist. For in the value system of civilization, of compulsive survival, the artist is irrelevant. He is seen as a mere decorator who entertains us while we labor. As strolling minstrel, player, clown, or poet he can pass everywhere because no one takes him seriously. "His language," says Marcuse, "is *song*, and his work is *play*."

Totalitarian states, however, know the danger of the artist. Correctly, if for the wrong reasons, they know that all art is propaganda, and that art which does not support their system must be against it. They know intuitively that the artist is not a harmless eccentric but one who under the guise of irrelevance creates and reveals a new reality. If, then, he is not to be torn to pieces like Orpheus in the myth, the liberative artist must be able to play the countergame and keep it as well hidden as the judo of Taoism and Zen. He must be able to be "all things to all men," for as one sees from the history of Zen any discipline whatsoever can be used as a way of liberation — making pots, designing gardens, arranging flowers, building houses, serving tea, and even using the sword; one does not have to advertise oneself as a psychotherapist or *guru*. He is the artist in whatever he does, not just in the sense of doing it beautifully, but in the sense of *playing* it. In the expressive lingo of the jazz world, whatever the scene, he makes it. Whatever he does, he *dances* it — like a Negro bootblack shining shoes. He swings.

It is not by chance that one thinks of the American Negro, his music and his language, in this connection. He retains the vestiges of a truly erotic culture, and it is this rather than his color and features which the Anglo-Saxon subculture so strongly resents. It is quite miraculous to listen to a Negro preacher and congregation convert the most unattractive Bible religion of the South into a swinging dance of superb nonsense. It is something of an exception to Jacob Boehme's feeling that

> ...no people understands any more the sensual language, and the birds in the air and the beasts in the forest do understand it according to their species. Therefore man may reflect what he has been robbed of, and what he is to recover in the second birth. For in the sensual language all spirits speak with each other, they need no other language, for it is the language of nature.[163]

I am not idealizing the Negro because, under the circumstances, his culture is no more than a vague glimmer of what I am trying to suggest, and it survives through overwhelming poverty and squalor. I am suggesting that it is possible to stop taking the universe and human life seriously by telling it that it *must* play, as if it were in course to some future ideal which it must reach at all costs. To feel this way is, indeed, to use the jazz lingo again, "a very far-out scene" — a way of being so intensely alienated that recovery will present an astonishing contrast.

The ways of liberation make it very clear that life is not going anywhere, because it is already *there*. In other words, it is playing, and those who do not play with it have simply missed the point. As Lewis Mumford puts it:

Beauty, for example, has played as large a part in evolution as use and cannot be explained, as Darwin sought to, merely as a practical device for courtship or fertilization. In short, it is just as permissible to conceive nature, mythologically, as a poet, working in metaphors and rhythms, as to think of nature as a cunning mechanic, trying to save material, make both ends meet, do the job efficiently and cheaply.[164]

The two views may be equally permissible in the sense that there is no reason why we may not play either, though to play that we are not playing leads to the vicious circles, frustrations, and contradictions of the double-bind — and *that* game is not worth the candle. It is to the degree that children play that they are not playing that "cops and robbers" leads to bloody noses and hurt feelings, and thus to the end of the game. Music, dancing, rhythm — all these are art forms which have no goal other than themselves, and to participate in them fully is to lay aside all thought of a *necessary* future; to say "must" to rhythm is to stop it dead. In the moment when he is anxious to play the correct notes, the musician is blocked. In both senses, he stops playing. He can perfect his art only by continuing to play, practicing without *trying* until the moment comes when he finds that the correct rhythm plays itself.

All perfect accomplishment in art or life is accompanied by the curious sensation that it is happening of itself — that it is not forced, studied, or contrived. This is not to say that everything which is felt to happen of itself is a perfect accomplishment; the marvel of human spontaneity is that it has developed the means of self-discipline — which becomes repressive only when it is felt that the controlling agent is separate from the action. But the sensation that the action is happening of itself, neither *from* an agent nor *to* a witness, is the authentic sensation of life as pure process, in which there is neither mover nor moved. Process without source or destination, verb without subject or object — this is not deprivation, as the word "without" suggests, but the "musical" sensation of arriving at every moment in which the melody and rhythm unfold.

Music is our nearest approximation to Boehme's "sensual language," for, unlike ordinary language, it does not refer to anything beyond itself, and though it has phrases and patterns, it is without sentences which separate subject from object, and parts of speech which separate things from events. "Abstract" as they may at first seem to be, music and pure mathematics are closer to life than are useful languages which point to meanings beyond themselves. Ordinary language refers to life, but music is living. But life itself is made to behave as ordinary language when it is lived for a purpose beyond itself, when the present serves the future, or when the body is exploited for the purposes of the soul. Such a way of life is therefore "beside itself" — insane — and because it is being made to behave as language and words it becomes as empty as "mere words." It has no recourse except to go on and on to the future to which the present apparently refers, only to find that here, too, the meaning is still beyond.

The liberative artist plays the part of Orpheus by living in the mode of music instead of the mode of language. His entire activity is dancing, rhythm for its own sake, and in this way he becomes a vortex which draws others into its pattern. He charms their attention from then to now, absorbing them into a rhythm in which survival ceases to be the criterion of value. It is by this attraction, and not by direction or commandment, that he is sought out as a teacher in the way of liberation. It is easy enough to become a martyr by throwing open challenges and judgments at the ways of the world. It is all too simple to indulge the sense of being in the right by flaunting one's lack of inhibition and scandalizing a repressed society. But the high art, the *upaya*, of a true bodhisattva is possible only for him who has gone beyond all need for self-justification; for so long as there is something to prove, some ax to grind, there is no dance.

From the standpoint of genuine liberation there are no inferior people. Because the ego never actually exists, those who are most captivated by its illusion are still playing. That they take it seriously and do not know that they are playing is honored by the bodhisattva as an extremely abandoned and risky game. For if the world *is* play there is no way of going against it. The most outright contradictions, the most firm assertions that the game is serious, the most absurd attempts to command spontaneity, and the most involved vicious circles can never be anything but extremely "far-out" forms of play. When it comes down to it, civilized repression simply builds up the power of Eros like water accumulating behind a dam. The game of hide-and-seek goes on because Eros continues to conceal and reveal itself in every rationalization, in the most deliberately spiritual and otherworldly images. Seeing this, the bodhisattva can never feel that he is condescending or that his liberation, his knowledge that the world is play, makes him superior to others. That he works for their liberation at all is only because of his compassion for them in the agony they feel when the game is unconscious, when seriousness is being played to an extreme. It is not so much the bodhisattva himself as the very extremity of the situation which generates compassion, for the most intense darkness is itself the seed of light, and all explicit warfare is implicit love.

Bibliographical References

1 A. W. Watts, *The Way of Zen* (New York: Pantheon, 1957).
2 P. Teilhard de Chardin, *The Phenomenon of Man* (New York: Harper, 1959), pp. 43–44.
3 J. Needham, *Science and Civilization in China*, Vol. 2 (Cambridge, UK: Cambridge University Press, 1956). See secs. 10, 13, 16, and 18.
4 *Cheng-tao ke*, 11, trans. D. T. Suzuki, *Manual of Zen Buddhism* (Kyoto: Eastern Buddhist Society, 1935), p. 108.
5 C. G. Jung, *Psychology and Religion: West and East*, Collected Works, Vol. 11, Bollingen Series 20 (New York: Pantheon, 1958), p. 476.
6 N. O. Brown, *Life against Death: The Psychoanalytical Meaning of History* (Middletown, CT: Wesleyan University Press, 1959), pp. 170–71.
7 R. Wilhelm and C. G. Jung, *The Secret of the Golden Flower* (London: Routledge, 1931), p. 83.
8 G. Murphy, *Personality: A Biosocial Approach to Origins and Structure* (New York: Harper, 1947).
9 A. F. Bentley, *Inquiry into Inquiries* (Boston: Beacon, 1954), p. 4.
10 L. Wittgenstein, *Tractatus Logico-Philosophicus* (London: Routledge, 1960), Sec. 6.37.
11 See reference 10, 6.371.
12 See reference 10, 6.5, 6.51, 6.52, 6.521.
13 J. Dewey and A. F. Bentley, *Knowing and the Known* (Boston: Beacon, 1949).
14 A. Angyal, *Foundations for a Science of Personality* (New York: Commonwealth Fund, 1941).

15 E. Brunswik, "Organismic Achievement and Environmental Probability," *Psychological Review*, Vol. 50, 1943.

16 See reference 8, p. 891.

17 See reference 10, 6.35.

18 *Tao Te Ching*, 2.

19 A. Strauss, ed., *The Social Psychology of George Herbert Mead* (Chicago: Phoenix, 1956).

20 See reference 19, pp. 257–58.

21 See reference 19, pp. 258–59.

22 See reference 19, p. 257n.

23 G. Bateson, with D. D. Jackson, J. Haley, and J. H. Weakland, "Towards a Theory of Schizophrenia," *Behavioral Science*, Vol. 1, 4, October 1956, pp. 251–64.

24 S. Radhakrishnan, *The Bhagavadgita* (New York: Harper, 1948), p. 177.

25 W. James, *A Pluralistic Universe* (New York: Longmans, 1909), p. 380.

26 From *Freud: The Mind of the Moralist* by Philip Rieff. Copyright © 1959 by Philip Rieff. Reprinted by permission of The Viking Press, Inc. Pp. 153–54.

27 E. Cassirer, *Substance and Function and Einstein's Theory of Relativity* (New York: Dover, 1953), p. 398.

28 G. Murphy, *Human Potentialities* (New York: Basic Books, 1958), p. viii.

29 T. R. V. Murti, *The Central Philosophy of Buddhism* (London: Allen and Unwin, 1955), p. 141.

30 See reference 10, 6.44, 6.522.

31 *Wu-men Kwan*, 49. P. Reps, *Zen Flesh, Zen Bones* (Rutland, VT, and Tokyo: Tuttle, 1957), p. 161.

32 A. David-Neel, *Secret Oral Teachings in the Tibetan Buddhist Sects* (Calcutta: Maha-Bodhi Society, n.d.), pp. 99–101.

33 See reference 32, pp. 101–2.

34 See reference 29, p. 167.

35 T. W. and C. A. F. Rhys Davids, trans., *Dialogues of the Buddha* (London: Luzac, 1951), Part II, p. 65.

36 A. K. Coomaraswamy, "Recollection Indian and Platonic, and The One and Only Transmigrant," Supplement to *Journal of the American Oriental Society*, Vol. 64, 2, 1937.

37 M. H. Erickson, J. Haley, and J. H. Weakland, "A Transcript of a Trance Induction with Commentary," *American Journal of Clinical Hypnosis*, Vol. 2, 2, 1959.

38 R. O. Kapp, *Towards a Unified Cosmology* (New York: Basic Books, 1960), pp. 57–58.

39 *Shih Niu T'ou*, 10.

40 Lin Yutang, *The Wisdom of Laotse* (New York: Random House, 1948), p. 41.

41 Ch'u Ta-kao, trans., *Tao Te Ching* (London: Buddhist Society, 1937), p. 44.

42 *Chuang-tzu*, 2. See reference 40, pp. 48–49.

43 *Chuang-tzu*, 13. H. A. Giles, trans., *Chuang Tzu* (Shanghai: Kelly and Walsh, 1926), pp. 166–67.

44 *Chuang-tzu*, 14. See reference 43, pp. 184–85.

45 *Chuang-tzu*, 4.

46 Chuang-tzu, 4.
47 Chuang-tzu, 22. See reference 43, p. 289.
48 Tao Te Ching, 18. See reference 41, p. 28.
49 Chuang-tzu, 6. See reference 43, pp. 69–70.
50 See reference 3, sec. 10, f and g.
51 Tao Te Ching, 23. See reference 41, p. 33, adjuv. auct.
52 Cf. D. T. Suzuki, Zen and Japanese Culture, Bollingen Series 64 (New York: Pantheon, 1959), Plates 1, 16, 58, 60, 63.
53 Chuang-tzu, 12. See reference 40, p. 129.
54 Chuang-tzu, 19. See reference 43, pp. 238–39.
55 D. T. Suzuki, Living by Zen (London: Rider, 1950), p. 137.
56 From The Cocktail Party, copyright 1950 by T. S. Eliot. Reprinted by permission of Harcourt, Brace & World, Inc., New York, 1952, p. 307.
57 A. W. Watts, This Is It (New York: Pantheon, 1960), final essay.
58 S. B. Dasgupta, Introduction to Tantric Buddhism (Calcutta: University of Calcutta, 1950).
59 M. Eliade, Yoga: Immortality and Freedom, Bollingen Series 58 (New York: Pantheon, 1958), esp. pp. 264–65.
60 J. Woodroffe, Shakti and Shakta (London: Luzac, 1929).
61 A. W. Watts, Nature, Man, and Woman (New York: Pantheon, 1958), pp. 190–95.
62 See reference 58, p. 203.
63 D. Snellgrove, trans., in E. Conze, ed., Buddhist Texts (Oxford: Cassirer, 1954), p. 226.
64 A. K. Coomaraswamy, The Dance of Shiva (New York: Noonday, 1957), pp. 124–34.
65 See reference 6.
66 See reference 64, p. 131.
67 R. Guénon, Introduction to the Study of the Hindu Doctrines (London: Luzac, 1945), p. 112.
68 See reference 6, p. 316.
69 G. Bachelard, La Formation de l'esprit scientifique (Paris: Librairie Philosophique J. Vrin, 1947), pp. 250–51.
70 G. Kepes, The New Landscape (Chicago: Theobald, 1956).
71 A. N. Whitehead, Adventures of Ideas (New York: Macmillan, 1933), pp. 322–23.
72 S. Freud, Civilization and Its Discontents (London: Hogarth, 1930), p. 144.
73 See reference 6, p. 322.
74 L. L. Whyte, The Next Development in Man (New York: Holt, 1948).
75 See reference 10, 5.5423.
76 See reference 71, p. 172.
77 R. May, Existence (New York: Basic Books, 1958), pp. 86–90.
78 G. Mora, "Recent American Psychiatric Developments," American Handbook of Psychiatry, 2 vols. (New York: Basic Books, 1960), p. 32.
79 See reference 5, p. 339.
80 S. Freud, Beyond the Pleasure Principle (London: Hogarth, 1955), p. 56.

81   See reference 72, pp. 121–22.

82   See reference 74, pp. 238–39.

83   S. Freud, *On Creativity and the Unconscious* (New York: Harper, 1958), pp. 55–62.

84   See reference 5, p. 484.

85   See reference 5, pp. 504–5.

86   See reference 7, p. 80.

87   C. G. Jung, *Modern Man in Search of a Soul* (London: Routledge, 1936), pp. 118–19.

88   A. H. Maslow, *Motivation and Personality* (New York: Harper, 1954), pp. 292–93.

89   See reference 88, pp. 291–92.

90   G. Groddeck, *The Book of the It* (London: C. W. Daniel, 1935) and *The World of Man* (London: C. W. Daniel, 1934).

91   W. Reich, *The Sexual Revolution* (New York: Orgone, 1945). Also, *Character Analysis* (New York: Orgone, 1949).

92   H. Marcuse, *Eros and Civilization* (Boston: Beacon, 1955).

93   See reference 6.

94   M. E. Harding, *Psychic Energy*, Bollingen Series 10 (New York: Pantheon, 1947), p. 1.

95   C. G. Jung, *The Development of Personality*, Collected Works, Vol. 17, Bollingen Series 20 (New York: Pantheon, 1954), p. 53.

96   See reference 57, Chap. 1.

97   See reference 52, p. 353.

98   *Lin-chi lü.*

99   Personal communication.

100 R. May, "The Existential Approach," *American Handbook of Psychiatry*, 2 vols. (New York: Basic Books, 1959), Vol. 2, p. 1349.

101 L. Binswanger, *Ausgewählte Vorträge und Aufsätze*, Bern, 1947. Quoted in reference 100.

102 See reference 77, pp. 18–19.

103 J. Ruesch and G. Bateson, *Communication: The Social Matrix of Psychiatry* (New York: Norton, 1951), Chap. 8.

104 See reference 55, p. 124.

105 See reference 6, pp. 104–5.

106 See reference 6, p. 106.

107 See reference 6, p. 92.

108 See reference 6, p. 93.

109 H. S. Sullivan, *The Interpersonal Theory of Psychiatry* (New York: Norton, 1953), p. 169.

110 H. S. Sullivan, "Tensions Interpersonal and International," in H. Cantril, ed., *Tensions That Cause War* (Urbana, IL: University of Illinois Press, 1950), p. 92.

111 J. Ruesch, *Disturbed Communication* (New York: Norton, 1957). J. Ruesch and W. Kees, *Nonverbal Communication* (Berkeley: University of California Press, 1956). See also reference 103.

112 G. Bateson, "The New Conceptual Frames for Behavioral Research," *Proceedings of the Sixth Annual Psychiatric Institute*, Princeton, 1958, pp. 54–71. See also reference 23.

113 A. Rapoport, "Mathematics and Cybernetics," *American Handbook of Psychiatry*, 2 vols. (New York: Basic Books, 1959), Vol. 2, p. 1743.

114 J. Haley, "The Art of Psychoanalysis," *ETC*, Vol. 15, 1958, pp. 190–200. Also, "Control in Psychoanalytic Psychotherapy," *Progress in Psychotherapy* (New York: Grune and Stratton, 1959).

115 J. Ruesch, "The Trouble with Psychiatric Research," *AMA Archives of Neurology and Psychiatry*, Vol. 77, 1957, p. 96.

116 G. Bateson, "Language and Psychotherapy," *Psychiatry*, Vol. 21, pp. 96 and 100.

117 E. Fromm, *The Sane Society* (New York: Rinehart, 1955), p. 143.

118 E. Fromm and D. T. Suzuki, *Zen Buddhism and Psychoanalysis* (New York: Harper, 1960).

119 See reference 116, pp. 99–100.

120 See reference 74, pp. 57 and 67.

121 See reference 114, "The Art of Psychoanalysis."

122 *Vajracchedika*, 22.

123 *Lin-chi lü*.

124 *Lin-chi lü*.

125 *Ku-tsun-hsü Yü-lu*, 1. 6.

126 E. Herrigel, *Zen in the Art of Archery* (New York: Pantheon, 1953).

127 *Wu-men kwan*, 14.

128 P. Reps, *Zen Flesh, Zen Bones* (Rutland, VT, and Tokyo: Tuttle, 1957).

129 D. T. Suzuki, *Essays in Zen Buddhism*, 3 vols. (London: Rider, 1949, 1950, 1951).

130 See reference 1.

131 A. J. Bahm, *The Philosophy of Buddha* (New York: Harper, 1958).

132 See reference 131, p. 98.

133 L. Giles, *Taoist Teachings* (London: Murray, 1925), pp. 40–42. Also in reference 1, p. 22.

134 See reference 1, pp. 93–94.

135 See reference 125, 1.2.4.

136 C. G. Jung, *The Integration of Personality* (New York: Rinehart, 1939), pp. 31–32.

137 See reference 92, pp. 168–69.

138 E. Erikson, *Young Man Luther* (New York: Norton, 1958), p. 264.

139 See reference 138, p. 263.

140 J. Haley, "Control in Psychoanalytic Psychotherapy," *Progress in Psychotherapy* (New York: Grune and Stratton, 1959), pp. 48–65.

141 F. S. Perls, R. F. Hefferline, and P. Goodman, *Gestalt Therapy* (New York: Julian Press, 1951), p. 259 and n.

142 J. Rosen, *Direct Analysis* (New York: Grune and Stratton, 1953).

143 See reference 140, p. 59.

144 *Hsin-hsin ming*. See reference 1, p. 115.

145 S. Freud, *New Introductory Lectures on Psychoanalysis* (New York: Norton, 1933), pp. 203–4.

146 Hakuin, *Zazen Wasan*. Cf. D. T. Suzuki in reference 4, p. 184.

147 See reference 6, p. 284.

148 See reference 6, p. 93.

149 See reference 6, pp. 158–59.

150 See reference 6, p. 307.

151 See reference 26, p. 355.

152 See reference 92, pp. 181–82.

153 C. B. Chisholm, "The Psychiatry of Enduring Peace and Social Progress," *Psychiatry*, Vol. 9, 1, 1946, p. 31.

154 See reference 92, p. 221.

155 See reference 26, p. 355.

156 R. LaPiere, *The Freudian Ethic* (New York: Duell, Sloan and Pierce, 1959).

157 A. M. Johnson, "Juvenile Delinquency," *American Handbook of Psychiatry*, 2 vols. (New York: Basic Books, 1959), Vol. 1, p. 840.

158 See reference 61, pp. 51–69.

159 See reference 3, sec. 18.

160 *Tao Te Ching*, 25.

161 *Chuang-tzu*, 23. In reference 40, pp. 85–86.

162 See reference 6, p. 46.

163 J. Boehme, *Mysterium Magnum*, Chap. 35.

164 L. Mumford, *The Conduct of Life* (New York: Harcourt, Brace, 1951), p. 35.

About the Author

Alan Watts, who held both a master's degree in theology and a doctorate of divinity, is best known as an interpreter of Zen Buddhism in particular, and of Indian and Chinese philosophy in general. Standing apart, however, from sectarian membership, he earned the reputation of being one of the most original and "unrutted" philosophers of the past century. He was the author of some twenty books on the philosophy and psychology of religion, including *The Way of Zen*; *The Wisdom of Insecurity*; *Nature, Man and Woman*; *The Book*; *Beyond Theology*; *In My Own Way*; and *Cloud-Hidden, Whereabouts Unknown*. He died in 1973.